Emerging New Voices in Critical Animal Studies: Vegan Studies for Total Liberation

"*Emerging New Voices in Critical Animal Studies: Vegan Studies for Total Liberation* is an important book because it gives space for new voices within social movements. This book is a book to hear the future goals and dreams, rather than demands and manifestos from veteran activists who are always on the mic. To protect the world, we must listen to our young people."

—Alisha Page, Director, Save the Kids

"This collection introduces emerging scholar-activists fighting for total liberation globally and proposes a new framework in which activists can use to create a global movement for social justice. In addition to its contribution to the field, *Emerging New Voices in Critical Animal Studies* offers ways for us to build solidarity with intersecting liberatory movements in order to dismantle all structures of oppression, domination, and hierarchy."

—Z. Zane McNeill, co-editor, *Queer and Trans Voices: Achieving Liberation Through Consistent Anti-Oppression*

"*Emerging New Voices in Critical Animal Studies* fosters new, critical dialogues and methods that encourage citizen-scholars and scholar-activists to reckon with humanity's past and present environmental, sociopolitical, and economic injustices. The collection interrogates how and why the injustices emerged and are reaffirmed through anthropocentrism and the cultural construction of human/animal, normal/abnormal, civilization/nature, normal/queer binary thinking that place a premium on some human life while devaluing the lives and possibilities of other humans and other species. Notably intersecting movements and critical theories, the co-editors and writers call readers to action by crossing their varied disciplinary approaches to build a collection that details for readers the necessary contexts and insights so that theory can be used to generate sustained action."

—Kati Lewis, Associate Professor, English, Salt Lake Community College

"This book is another masterful critical animal studies compilation of research and essays dedicated to the liberation of all beings. The question of why some of us are free and some of us exist only to serve others has yet to be fully answered and understood. The journey toward that answer and the impending liberation of all, continues with this excellent work."

—Dr. John Alessio, author, *Social Problems and Inequality*

"*Emerging New Voices in Critical Animal Studies* is an outstanding cutting-edge profound book that is a must read for anyone that cares about animals and social justice. This engaging powerful text forces the reader to rethink how they live in relation to the exploitation of the world. This book pushes us closer to a more harmonious, balanced, ecologically interdependent peaceful planet."

—*Peace Studies Journal*

"*Emerging New Voices in Critical Animal Studies* is a great addition to the ever-growing canon of critical animal studies texts. The authors approach total liberation from multidisciplinary, transnational perspectives ranging from theological inquiry to Turkish governmental policy. It is an important read for anyone interested in global human and nonhuman animal liberation."

—Dr. S. Marek Muller, Assistant Professor, Rhetorical Studies,
Florida Atlantic University

"One of the greatest contributions of critical animal studies has been to create a space for activists and activist-scholars to be seen and heard, and taken seriously. *Emerging New Voices in Critical Animal Studies* is a powerful reflection of—and testament to—this ongoing commitment. This is a collection which enriches our knowledge and understanding with originality and verve."

—Dr. Richard J. White, Reader in Human Geography,
Sheffield Hallam University, UK

"This powerful and essential new work features some of the emerging and diverse voices of the latest generation of CAS scholar/activists. Their profound insights and visions, grounded in the critical animal studies tradition, are invaluable in the ongoing struggle against all forms of oppression."

—Dr. David Nibert, Professor of Sociology, Wittenberg University

"*Emerging New Voices in Critical Animal Studies* creates a new paradigm in the study of sovereignty, human-efficacy, and the anti-imperialist promotion of things in the current Anthropocene epoch. The book presents scholars that have proved themselves greatly to create and promote solidarity through intersectional loci. The totality of many oppressions can be dissected and understood greatly through these works."

—Lucas Alan Dietsche, Editor-in-Chief, *Transformative Justice Journal*

"*Emerging New Voices in Critical Animal Studies* is a door opener to a much-needed new dialogue platform, looking at the way forward and preserving our future. At the end of the day, there will be opposing groups in a room charting the way forward. The narrative of this book needs to be at the table of dialogue."

—Dr. Clyde Rivers, Founder, iChange Nations

"*Emerging New Voices in Critical Animal Studies* will take readers on a crucial emotional journey as they highlight current atrocities happening around the world. The content is very engaging and thought provoking—leaving you respecting how you live your life or with an action list of things you must change. An essential read for all people."

—J. Ellis, Adjunct Faculty, Criminal Justice, Salt Lake Community College

"Poirier, Bernatchez, and Nocella have put together a brilliant critical text that will expand the fields of intersectionality, social justice, and sociology within the realms of animal ethics, critical animal studies, posthumanism, and animalia."

—Dr. Erik Juergensmeyer, Editor, *Green Theory and Praxis Journal*

Emerging New Voices
in Critical Animal Studies

RADICAL ANIMAL STUDIES AND TOTAL LIBERATION

Anthony J. Nocella II
Series Editor

Vol. 10

The Radical Animal Studies and Total Liberation series
is part of the Peter Lang Education list.
Every volume is peer reviewed and meets
the highest quality standards for content and production.

PETER LANG
New York • Bern • Berlin
Brussels • Vienna • Oxford • Warsaw

Emerging New Voices in Critical Animal Studies

Vegan Studies for Total Liberation

Edited by
Nathan Poirier, Anthony J. Nocella II,
and Annie Bernatchez

PETER LANG
New York • Bern • Berlin
Brussels • Vienna • Oxford • Warsaw

Library of Congress Cataloging-in-Publication Data

Names: Poirier, Nathan, editor. | Nocella, Anthony J., editor. |
Bernatchez, Annie, editor.
Title: Emerging new voices in critical animal studies: vegan studies for
total liberation / Nathan Poirier, Anthony J. Nocella II, Annie Bernatchez.
Description: New York: Peter Lang, 2022.
Series: Radical animal studies and total liberation; vol. 10
ISSN 2469-3065 (print) | ISSN 2469-3081 (online)
Includes bibliographical references and index.
Identifiers: LCCN 2021051307 (print) | LCCN 2021051308 (ebook) |
ISBN 978-1-4331-9287-6 (hardback) | ISBN 978-1-4331-9169-5 (paperback) |
ISBN 978-1-4331-9166-4 (ebook) | ISBN 978-1-4331-9167-1 (epub)
Subjects: LCSH: Animal rights—Political aspects. | Animal
welfare—Political aspects. | Veganism—Political aspects. | Social
justice. | Speciesism.
Classification: LCC HV4708 .E49 2022 (print) | LCC HV4708 (ebook) |
DDC 179/.3—dc23/eng/20211019
LC record available at https://lccn.loc.gov/2021051307
LC ebook record available at https://lccn.loc.gov/2021051308
DOI 10.3726/b19252

Bibliographic information published by **Die Deutsche Nationalbibliothek.**
Die Deutsche Nationalbibliothek lists this publication in the "Deutsche
Nationalbibliografie"; detailed bibliographic data are available
on the Internet at http://dnb.d-nb.de/.

Dedication

This book is dedicated to everyone that fights for total liberation and against fascism, oppression, and domination. This book is also dedicated to protests against—Trump, union busting organizations, universities that put their students in debt, the military industrial complex, and those who destroy nature with their sports such skiing, ATVs, and water skiing. This book is also dedicated to student activists around the world fighting for academic freedom and against academic repression. We would like to extend a particular dedication to those murdered by police brutality, the humans and nonhumans who have died because of COVID-19, and those who froze to death in southern United States.

Table of Contents

Acknowledgments

We the editors (Anthony J. Nocella II, Nathan Poirier, and Annie Bernatchez) of this book would like to thank first the contributors within this book—Sean Parson, Kati Lewis, Allison Gray, Maryline El Khoury, Kenzo Jacquemin, Alaina Interisano, Sarah Tomasello, Annie Bernatchez, Deniz Hosbay Bayraktar, Ozgur Bayraktar, and Will Boisseau. We would also like to thank the publisher Peter Lang Publishing and those that work with the publisher such as Jackie Pavlovic, Patty Mulrane, Dani Green, and Preetha Ambat. We would also like to thank those that wrote reviews for the book: Z. Zane McNeill, Kati Lewis, Peace Studies Journal, Dr. S. Marek Muller, Dr. Richard J. White, Dr. David Nibert, Lucas Alan Dietsche, Dr. Clyde Rivers, J. Ellis, and Dr. Erik Juergensmeyer. This book would not be possible if not for the organizations and academic departments that support our scholarship and activism such as Save the Kids, Academy for Peace Education, Utah Reintegration Project, Ecoability Collective, Journal for Critical Animal Studies, Lowrider Studies Book Series, Arissa Media Group, Poetry Behind the Walls, Wisdom Behind the Walls, Durango Peace and Justice, Salt Lake Peace and Justice, Green Theory and Praxis Journal, Transformative Justice Journal, Department of Criminal Justice at Salt Lake Community College, Peace Studies Journal, Institute for Critical Animal Studies, Academy for Critical Animal Studies, Critical Animal Studies Society, Lowrider Studies Journal, and Journal of Hip Hop Studies. Finally, would like to thank our friends and family.

In particular, Nathan would like to thank Tom Dietz and Linda Kalof for providing scholarly direction to help protect nonhuman animals and the environment, those involved at the Institute for Critical Animal Studies for their tireless work that aims to bring about total liberation of which this book is a small part, my partner Erin for selflessly putting up with me (still) attending graduate school while she works a full-time office job, and my parents for being ever supportive of my lifelong ambitions in whatever direction they have taken.

Foreword

SEAN PARSON

Writing at the, hopefully, end of a pandemic is different than it was before. Like all social, political, and ecological crises, the COVID-19 pandemic highlighted the tensions that already existed in our society and brought them to the fore. For instance, during the year 2020, it is estimated that the world's billionaires saw a jaw-dropping 54% increase in their wealth. While most people struggled financially, as job losses peaked and governments did little to protect working folks, and emotionally, as the weight of well over 3.5 million dead haunt the memory of the living. Mothers, daughters, sons, neighbors, friends, strangers have died in mass during this last year. Sadly, the crippling economic and psychological costs of the year are more an example of things to come with the catastrophic aspects of climate change only worsening each year, as economic inequality grows to record levels and as neo-fascist political mobilizations grow throughout the world. We are at a time—and maybe we always are—in which what we collectively do now lays bare whether we ended up with, as Rosa Luxemburg famously said, "socialism or barbarism." Yet, in the public debates and discussion for the future—especially in mainstream media and in most leftist sources—this question is always centered around the quality of life of humans. The nonhuman animals are erased from the discussion. Primarily because for nonhuman animals whose bodies are bred, raised, and slaughtered for the benefit of human animals' barbarism has been the norm.

For instance, on average, around nine billion chickens are murdered in the United States alone. The mass graves of chicken bones are so extensive that these remains will be one of the "artifacts" of the Anthropocene—the new geological era defined by the global impact of the human species on planetary systems. These mass graves, along with plastics and radiation, will trace the marks of industrial Capitalism for millennia. Yet, this devastation was promoted and benefited only a tiny subset of the human species. Indigenous populations, the global south, and poor and destitute in the so-called North experience a disproportionate amount of the violence from industrial Capitalism but are often excluded from the benefits. In a system where profit and accumulation are all that matter, life—both human and non—are commodified. This opens the space for everyone to become a potential sacrifice to the gods of Capitalism.

Yet, the human violence to nonhumans inevitably cycles back to impact humans as well. Life is, in fact, interconnected. We cannot alter or destroy a part of our world without everyone experiencing the repercussions of that violence. This interconnection is dangerous for capitalism, as it knows that for it to exploit us all, it needs to isolate and alienate. Following the dictates and logic of neoliberal Capitalism there is pressure to focus our attention on only our own well-being, our own branding, and our own liberation. What is lost with this mindset is that old wobbly slogan, "An Injury to One is an Injury to All."

An example is the development of covid. While there is debate, and conspiracy theory accusations, about the origin of Covid, the most likely outcome, given the scientific evidence so far, is that the virus is zoogenic, meaning it spread from a nonhuman animal to a human animal. The most likely culprits are either bats or pangolins. The spreading of diseases from nonhuman animals to human animals is not new, but the process is intensified by industrial animal agriculture and the expansion of human development into natural areas worldwide. Thus, the horrific violence of industrial animal agriculture is, thus, in large part, to blame for the global pandemic. Yet, like most topics, the animal question gets erased. What goes around comes around. The pandemic, not often framed this way, is a lesson in the importance of a total liberation approach. Human liberation is linked to animal liberation, and both require ecological justice.

This was a long way to get to the importance and value of this book. Critical animal studies has been a leading voice analyzing and resisting the commodification of life and industrial capitalism's barbarism. Unlike most academic fields or disciplines, critical animal studies has always centered praxis. The work is not purely intellectual or performative, which sadly most academic work is. As an approach to critical theory, CAS calls on the scholars to be activists and on the activists to be a scholar. It also, unlike a lot of well-funded nonprofit oriented animal rights organizations—like PETA—understands the complexity of modern life under industrial Capitalism, Racial Capitalism, and settler colonialism and advocates for an anti-capitalism that centers not just animal liberation but the abolition of white supremacy, patriarchy, militarism, settler colonialism, ableism, and all other destructive structures that cause violence and limit flourishing and happiness for all. Critical animal studies adds an essential voice to the debates that happen in the halls of academia, among individuals strategizing actions inspired by the ELF and ALF, and in the consensus meetings of activists in parks and community centers. The new voices in this book are an example of the activist-scholar and scholar-activist that makes CAS unique. We also see the injection of a new spirit, new focus, new passion, and new ideas. These ideas do not come just from the classrooms—as we see way too often in academia—but from people committed to the work on the ground. Their experiences and deep passions made this book happen, and it's those passions and activist projects that make CAS the powerful voice it is.

The future is always unwritten, but the elites of the world are hellbent on maintaining their power as the authors. The story they want to write is one in which the ravages of climate change are met, not with mutual aid and liberation, but fascistic and neo-feudal capitalism. They want a world in which those who are reaping the benefits of exploitation and violence today will be the same ones thriving. This book, like the field of CAS in general, is part of a broader movement to change the future. To try to imagine and create a world in which nonhuman animals are not victim to systemic violence and industrial murder and where all living beings are able to thrive, flourish, and find community and purpose.

Preface

KATI LEWIS

Emerging New Voices in Critical Animal Studies: Vegan Studies for Total Liberation renders quite clearly and starkly injustices driven by anthropocentrism as it centers on medical, livestock, and academic pursuits that perpetuate the animal industrial complex and speciesist capitalist domination. This collection of essays investigates the damage engineered by upholding binary thinking about humans/animals and the "civilized" world/natural world—binaries which have, for millennia, perpetuated the exploitative ideology that animals have value only in relationship to the monetary and "health" benefits that they provide humans. Animals have a right to exist absent their profit-making abilities for humans. The critical reframing of humanity as just one part of a complex, rhizomorphic ecosphere is one transformative through line in the collection.

While the book includes a diverse range of methods and approaches for utilizing theory for action, each essay takes up a biocentric argument for how humans must move forward in the contexts of climate change, the COVID-19 pandemic, and increasing inequality as we grapple with the human-driven mass extinction of species currently and irreparably creating colossal loss of biodiversity. The writers call to account institutions ranging from academia to the animal-industrial complex for reinforcing and abetting the continued evisceration of animal rights even as plant-based diets become increasingly normalized. Thus, readers are encouraged to take the facts contextualized via the lens of Critical Animal Studies (CAS) and use them to advance radical change individually and collectively. Indeed, this collection would not be possible without the galvanizing actions of Students for Critical Animal Studies, actions which include animal liberation as a fundamental part of radical social change in which hierarchies are dismantled and societies are structured with and in community for the benefit of the ecosphere.

From more personal and professional positions—I am a community college Queer Studies professor—I read the collection from the lenses of CAS and queer ecology. I came out bisexual during fall 2015 as a response to mandate from the Church of Jesus Christ of Latter-Day Saints' (LDS) that sought to further divide families that included LGBTQIA2+ human beings and to reinforce anti-queer ideologies in a campaign that further monsterized and othered non-straight, gender-nonconforming people within its sphere of influence. I followed up my coming out with officially demanding that my name be removed from the LDS church's record, making me an apostate as well as someone "choosing a 'counterfeit lifestyle.'" Being queer, you see, is not a legitimate, genuine identity to the community I was born and raised in. The language surrounding queer people and communities during European colonization, especially during the Victorian era, remains very much a part of the right-wing and evangelical discourses. Undergirded by dividing people into normal/abnormal and natural/unnatural binaries, these discourses cast queer human beings as outside of nature, casting us outside of the natural world. (The religion of my youth also engages in domination-model mixed with the care-taking model of humanity's role on the planet).

In thinking about queer identities in relation to this collection's examination of human animal- and nonhuman animal-centered issues with their attendant environmental implications, I'm reminded of a fundamental tenet of queer ecology: human beings impact and are impacted by other species. Everything is connected. In this reciprocal relationship, there has always-already been a spectrum of queerness—queerness that fosters biodiversity and possibility. Rather than competitive, queerness is communal and collaborative. Queer ecology is grounded in enthusiastic resistance against the regimes of the norm constructed by the capitalist, ableist, cishet, white patriarchy. This kind of grounding is not new, Indigenous and other communities of color have shaped these community-based frameworks for transformative change and justice and it would be another form of erasure and appropriation to not emphasis these realities.

As I attempt to conclude the preface—a preface that feels more like a reflection on the memories that the collection of essays has called up for me—I feel the obligation to share another tenet of queer ecology, which is to critique identity. The foundation of *Emerging New Voices in Critical Animal Studies: Vegan Studies for Total Liberation* is CAS. For me, its subtext is queer ecology. Its purposes are to warn us about where we've been and we're at in the continuing cycle of brutality against animals and it's also to be revelatory. The individual essays in this collection and the collection taken as a body of research demands that we critique how we've framed our identities in the ecosphere and urges us resist the regimes of the hegemonic norms fueling crisis after crisis. Its project is introspection leading to action. We must listen to the warnings, take in the revelations, and embrace the hope and change that is possible if we act—together.

Dismantling Speciesism for Total Liberation

NATHAN POIRIER, ANNIE BERNATCHEZ,
AND ANTHONY J. NOCELLA II

BACKGROUND

This book emerged out of the 2020 Students for Critical Animal Studies Conference (SCAS) co-hosted by Nathan Poirier and Annie Bernatchez, during the fight for Black Lives Matter globally, on the heels of Standing Rock (Estes, 2019; Gilio-Whitaker, 2020) and as CAS fought for racial justice (Kendi, 2019). This book also emerged as millions of animals were killed because of COVID-19 and humans were deliberately endangered (Kevany, 2020a; Kevany, 2020b) due to grievous and purposive mismanagement by Donald Trump and other elites. This book contains chapters by some of those who presented at SCAS in 2020, and a couple additional entries by other graduate students. The conception of this book is a novelty for Critical Animal Studies (CAS) in that it is the first book to be dedicated solely to students who are scholar-activists within the CAS tradition. In doing this, the present book, as well as the conference it is derived from, are tangible outcomes of part of CAS's mission to help emerging activists and scholars gain experience and promote their work. In this way, CAS not only helps foster an intersectional approach to total liberation—liberation of human and nonhuman animals and the environment—but also welcomes younger scholars who will inevitably bring new and different perspectives to the field of CAS (Pellow, 2014; Nocella, Drew, George, Ketenci, Lupinacci, Purdy, & Schatz, 2019). Two of the editors, Annie and Nathan, have been fortunate beneficiaries of this part of CAS outreach having had the opportunities to organize a conference, gain experience in writing and editing, as well as participate in activism as part of a larger community of CAS and its wide network of affiliations and ally groups. Thus, part of the goal of this book is to help pay these benefits forward to help in publishing works from presenters in the SCAS 2020 conference. Helping create a platform for emerging and marginalized voices (such as women, People of Color, youth, indigenous, people with disabilities, LGBTQ+, and non-U.S. citizens) contributes towards decolonizing and radicalizing pedagogy and activism as it allows more and often underrepresented voices to be heard and helps foster confidence for students to use their own critical ideas and approaches in their own schools, classrooms, activism, and lives (Harper, 2010; Nocella, Bentley & Duncan, 2012; Socha, 2012; Ko & Ko, 2017; Brueck, 2017, 2019; Adewale, 2021). Students reading this are encouraged to become involved with the Institute for Critical Animal Studies (ICAS) and SCAS by submitting proposals for presentations or publications to any one of ICAS's many events held throughout the year and publishing outlets. See criticalanimalstudies.org for frequent updates on CAS events, calls for book chapters, and other ways to be involved in scholar-activism for total liberation against all forms of domination and oppression such as capitalism and colonialism (Colling, 2021).

GOAL OF THE BOOK

Critical animal studies is an activist movement and scholarly field founded by Anthony J. Nocella II, Steve Best, John Sorenson, and Richard Kahn, with support from others, in 2006. Critical animal studies promotes education not schooling, and scholars not academics. Critical animal studies is grounded in intersectionality (Crenshaw, 1989), total liberation, and anarchism. Many people claim to be or to do critical animal studies, but do not support these theoretical frameworks, which actually makes them ignorant of the field and movement (Nocella & George, 2019). On the other hand, some scholars who write critically of human-animal relations, such as Carol J. Adams, Giorgio Agamben, and J. M. Coetzee, frequently have their work labeled as critical animal studies but they do not actually support the principles of CAS (see below) and in some cases are actually against the mission of CAS. We do not doubt such scholars' commitment to creating more hospitable living situations for non/humans, but we simply aim to clarify that CAS has a specific vision that is frequently misrepresented from the outside, whether consciously or not. Moreover, those that claim to be for animal liberation, but identify as animal studies scholars, are lacking in research or historical conceptualization, as animal studies was coined by vivisectors and animal testers in the 1960s. CAS is opposed to animal experimentation in all forms and therefore also distances itself from animal studies.

Critical animal studies is a growing global field, but with many opportunists, careerists, and co-opters. We must challenge these individuals to be activists and radical. To be clear, critical animal studies does not emerge out of animal studies or Human-Animal Studies (Nocella, Sorenson, Socha, & Matsuoka, 2014). Human-animal studies is theoretical vivisection from a critical animal studies perspective as the field does not argue for animal liberation, total liberation, or social justice, it is merely a detached apolitical objectivist anti-narrative, intellectual exercise of examination, not analysis of any past, present, or future fictional or factual relationship between humans and nonhuman animals. We could not think of a more useless field than Human-Animal Studies, one that has no purpose beyond examination. Examination is the viewing of a subject, topic, or issue only on the surface and externally, while analysis is the viewing of a subject, topic or issue on the surface as well as within its social context and in a case-study comparison to other subjects, topics, and issues. Silence is violence as we see animal studies and human-animal studies as just that—silence in the face of oppression. All scholarship and activism must be done for total liberation, justice, peace, freedom, and anarchy. This is why, as opposed to animal studies or human-animal studies, CAS openly supports the mission and actions of such radical groups as the Animal Liberation Front (Best & Nocella, 2004) and Earth Liberation Front (Best & Nocella, 2006; Nocella et al., 2019). Critical animal studies is for anarchism and against all forms of oppression and domination, including capitalism and colonialism (Best, Kahn, Nocella II, & McLaren, 2011; Albert & Chomsky, 2014; Nibert, 2017; White, 2017).

In 2007, Best, Nocella, Kahn, Carol Gigliotti, and Lisa Kemmerer, developed "The Ten Principles of Critical Animal Studies," which follow here:

1. Pursues interdisciplinary collaborative writing and research in a rich and comprehensive manner that includes perspectives typically ignored by animal studies such as political economy.
2. Rejects pseudo-objective academic analysis by explicitly clarifying its normative values and political commitments, such that there are no positivist illusions whatsoever that theory is disinterested or writing and research is nonpolitical. To support experiential understanding and subjectivity.
3. Eschews narrow academic viewpoints and the debilitating theory-for-theory's sake position in order to link theory to practice, analysis to politics, and the academy to the community.
4. Advances a holistic understanding of the commonality of oppressions, such that speciesism, sexism, racism, ableism, statism, classism, militarism and other hierarchical ideologies and institutions are viewed as parts of a larger, interlocking, global system of domination.

5. Rejects apolitical, conservative, and liberal positions in order to advance an anti-capitalist, and, more generally, a radical anti-hierarchical politics. This orientation seeks to dismantle all structures of exploitation, domination, oppression, torture, killing, and power [by humans to each other and other animals] in favor of decentralizing and democratizing society at all levels and on a global basis.

6. Rejects reformist, single-issue, nation-based, legislative, strictly animal interest politics in favor of alliance politics and solidarity with other struggles against oppression and hierarchy.

7. Champions a politics of total liberation which grasps the need for, and the inseparability of, human, nonhuman animal, and Earth liberation and freedom for all in one comprehensive, though diverse, struggle.

8. Deconstructs and reconstructs the socially constructed binary oppositions between human and nonhuman animals, a move basic to mainstream animal studies, but also looks to illuminate related dichotomies between culture and nature, civilization and wilderness and other dominator hierarchies to emphasize the historical limits placed upon humanity, nonhuman animals, cultural/political norms, and the liberation of nature as part of a transformative project that seeks to transcend these limits towards greater freedom, peace, and ecological harmony.

9. Openly supports and examines controversial radical politics and strategies used in all kinds of social justice movements, such as those that involve economic sabotage from boycotts to direct action toward the goal of peace.

10. Seeks to create openings for constructive critical dialogue on issues relevant to Critical Animal Studies across a wide-range of academic groups; citizens and grassroots activists; the staffs of policy and social service organizations; and people in private, public, and non-profit sectors. Through – and only through — new paradigms of ecopedagogy, bridge-building with other social movements, and a solidarity-based alliance politics, it is possible to build the new forms of consciousness, knowledge, and social institutions that are necessary to dissolve the hierarchical society that has enslaved this planet for the last ten thousand years. (pp. 4–5)

In an age of rising fascism and climate change—both on the global scale—these principles are more important now than ever. It is imperative that people come together, celebrate differences and find solidarity through commonalities in a united struggle for justice. Anyone can be an activist and an activist can come from anywhere. It is important to recognize that everyone can do *something*. Fascism harms even some fascists, just like patriarchy also harms some men. While climate change does not harm all evenly, it does affect everyone, human and non-human. When the singular goal of the powerful is to remain in their position by any means necessary—and they will consolidate and pull together to protect a generalized "elite" status—so too must the oppressed be willing to stand together in recognizing one struggle for freedom and to pursue freedom by creative and radical means as necessary. We must not lose sight of the micropolitics of oppression, everyday interactions and those who are suffering now. But we must also retain a large-scale vision of structures that allow small scale acts of domination to continue and to aim our actions at dismantling those structures. Incrementalism and reform simply will not cut it. Because the sources and forces of domination are all interrelated (Best et al., 2011), so too must the means of resistance.

In part, this entails recognizing and acknowledging our privileges as individuals and as collectives (i.e., all white people benefit to some degree from white privilege). Those with privilege can use it to help out the less advantaged, or else stop using their privilege(s) to their own advantage.

OUTLINE OF THE BOOK

This critical, powerful, insightful and important contribution to critical animal studies is filled with new brilliant scholar-activists fighting for social justiceand total liberation grounded in anarchism and intersectionality (Crenshaw, 1989). Contributors cover a range of issues, sometimes within a single chapter. They do so with different voices and perspectives, based in different social and geographical locations. But all challenge authority and the status quo. The following is a short overview of each chapter in the book.

Chapter One, "When the Animal-Industrial Complex Grows … Leaves," by Allison Gray, critically questions the ability of "meat" made from all plant ingredients to aid in total liberation. Alison notes a qualitative difference between plant-meat and *in vitro* meat that gives plant-meat an advantage in terms of greater potential for total liberation as these products are materially animal free. However, Allison also shows how plant-meat is at least partially emerging within the animal industrial complex which will have significant effects in terms of the ability for plant-meat to make disruptive systemic change.

Chapter Two, "Agency and Suffering in Animal Studies and in Animal Liberation," written by Maryline El Khoury and Kenzo Jacquemin, is about how mainstream animal studies (the general field of exploring human-animal relations) is insufficient for empowering animals and politicizing animal liberation. As part of this, Maryline and Kenzo suggest what they see as a more appropriate and radical approach to animal liberation, one that pays closer attention to the tactics used by nonhuman animals themselves. Using a theory-to-practice approach to effective activism, the authors pay special attention to how mainstream and radical activism differ in their use of the notions of power, agency, resistance, and suffering.

Chapter Three, "'It's a Privilege': A Critical Examination of University Students' Perspectives of Animal Experimentation in Science Education," by Alaina Interisano, uses critical animal pedagogy to show how students are socialized into viewing nonhuman animals as objects to be manipulated for human benefit(s). Alaina illuminates how institutional procedures, such as a speciesist pedagogy that teaches animal experimentation, becomes internalized as comfortable and the preferred way of relating to nonhumans which fosters an unwillingness to change practices. Alaina's suggestion is to move away from mainstream Western education to a critical animal pedagogy.

Chapter Four, "Nonhuman 'Others': A Theology of Hope and Liberation," written by Sarah Tomasello, draws on liberation theology as a means by which to integrate human and nonhuman animal liberation. Originating in Latin America in the 1960s, and having expanded globally as other marginalized groups organized their own theologies of liberation, Sarah sees liberation theology as compatible with critical animal studies in that both constitute radical systemic critiques of the status quo. In doing this, Sarah contributes to the discussion within and outside of CAS (for example, Leo Tolstoy's commitment to vegetarianism and a peaceful, Christian anarchism) about whether religion is itself a system of domination or if it can be used as a means to effect intersectional total liberation.

Chapter Five, "The V-Stamp as an Indirect Crime Against the Animals," written by one of the editors and co-organizer of the 2020 SCAS conference Annie Bernachez, is about the institutional and systemic harms wrought upon animals by the veterinary industry. Careful to point out that while many individual veterinarians care deeply for animals, administrative veterinarians often operate in speciesist ways. Terming the perceived authority behind veterinarian-approved policies and procedures the "V-Stamp," Annie shows how welfare measures within veterinary science and practice normalize the use and abuse of animals' bodies by legitimizing acceptable levels of harm.

Chapter Six, "The Phaeton Conflict in Turkey: The Case of Animal Domination in Instanbul Adalar," by Deniz Hosbay Bayraktar, analyzes grassroots activism in Turkey against the use of phaetons—horse drawn carriages. This chapter nuances animal liberation strategies from a non-Western perspective. Through examining the social situation concerning phaetons in Instanbul, Turkey—media articles, phaeton operators, city inhabitants, the government, and animal rights activists—Deniz reveals the speciesist and neoliberal ideologies of phaeton use and the ultimately successful efforts to abolish the practice.

Chapter Seven, "A Comparison of the Local Governments in Terms of Approaches to Stray Animals in Turkey," by Deniz Hosbay Bayraktar and Ozgur Bayraktar, is about how left- and right-wing municipal governments in Turkey approached the issue of feral animals. Deniz and Ozgur find that right-wing municipalities are more hostile and aggressive towards stray animals, and left-wing municipalities are much more respecting of the animals' right to life and care. This chapter complements Deniz's previous chapter in that it also examines Turkish animal activism, critically evaluating strategy in light of total liberation.

This book is not a complete collection of voices within critical animal studies, but we believe in and support these voices, those who fight for social justice, animal liberation, and total liberation grounded in anarchism and intersectionality (Nocella, Shannon & Asimakopoulos, 2012; Nocella, White & Cudworth, 2015; White & Springer, 2018). Justice and liberation can only be possible if we provide space and place for new voices and do not dominate or exploit those spaces and places for ego or economic benefit. Editing publications such as journals and books and organizing educational events such as conferences is essential for social change, but is difficult because editing and organizing requires collaboration with others. Collaboration can be difficult but also beautiful as it allows those involved to educate, learn, reflect, develop, act, take accountability and responsibility, and sometimes even heal. The voices contained in this volume represent a continuing of the CAS tradition established by Best et al. (2007) and Nocella et al. (2014). In this sense, these are not new voices replacing the old but building on what has come before. May all those who read these radical works be inspired to resist oppression in all its forms in a collective effort to build a better tomorrow for, and in solidarity with, all.

REFERENCES

Adewale, O.. (2021). *Brotha vegan: Black men speak on food, identity, health, and society.* Lantern Books.

Albert, M., & Chomsky, N. (2014). *Realizing hope: Life beyond capitalism.* Zed Books.

Best, S., & Nocella, A. J. (Eds.). (2004). *Terrorists or freedom fighters?: Reflections on the liberation of animals.* Lantern Books.

Best, S., & Nocella II, A. J. (Eds.). (2006). *Igniting a revolution: Voices in defense of the earth.* AK Press.

Best, S., Nocella, A. J., Kahn, R., Gigliotti, C., & Kemmerer, L. (2007). The ten principles of critical animal studies. *Journal for Critical Animal Studies, 5*(1), 4–5.

Best, S., Kahn, R., Nocella II, A. J., & McLaren, P. (Eds.). (2011). *The global industrial complex: Systems of domination.* Lexington Books.

Brueck, J. F. (2017). *Veganism in an oppressive world: A vegans-of-color community project.* Sanctuary Publishers.

Brueck, J. F. (2019). *Veganism of color: Decentering whiteness in human and nonhuman Liberation.* Sanctuary Publishers.

Colling, S. (2021). *Animal resistance in the global capitalist era.* Michigan State University Press.

Crenshaw, K. (1989). Demarginalizing the intersection of race and sex: A Black feminist critique of antidiscrimination doctrine. *University of Chicago Legal Forum,* 139–168.

Estes, N. (2019). *Our history is the future: Standing Rock versus the Dakota Access Pipeline, and the long tradition of indigenous resistance.* Verso.

Gilio-Whitaker, D. (2020). *As long as grass grows: The indigenous fight for environmental justice, from colonization to Standing Rock.* Beacon Press.

Harper, B. A. (2010). *Sistah vegan: Black female vegans speak on food, identity, health, and society.* Lantern Books.

Kendi, I. X. (2019). *How to be an anti-racist.* One World.

Kevany, S. (2020a). Millions of US farm animals to be culled by suffocation, drowning and shooting. *The Guardian* Tuesday 19 May. https://www.theguardian.com/environment/2020/may/19/millions-of-us-farm-animals-to-be-culled-by-suffocation-drowning-and-shooting-coronavirus

Kevany, S. (2020b). A million mink culled in Netherlands and Spain amid Covid-19 fur farming havoc. *The Guardian.* https://www.theguardian.com/world/2020/jul/17/spain-to-cull-nearly-100000-mink-in-coronavirus-outbreak

Ko, A., & Ko, S. (2017). *Aphro-ism: Essays on pop culture, feminism, and black veganism from two sisters.* Lantern Books.

Nibert, D. (2017). *Animal oppression and capitalism.* Praeger.

Nocella II, A. J., & George, A. E. (2019). *Intersectionality of critical animal studies: A historical collection.* Peter Lang Publishing.

Nocella II, A. J., Bentley, K. C., & Duncan, J. M. (2012). *Earth, animal, and disability liberation: The rise of the eco-ability movement.* Peter Lang.

Nocella II, A. J., Shannon, D., & Asimakopoulos, J. (2012). *The accumulation of freedom: Writings on anarchist economics.* AK Press.

Nocella II, A. J., Sorenson, J., Socha, K., & Matsuoka, A. (2014). *Defining critical animal studies: An intersectional social justice approach for liberation.* Peter Lang.

Nocella II, A. J., White, R. J., & Cudworth, E. (2015). *Anarchism and animal liberation: Essays on complementary aspects of total liberation.* McFarland Press.

Nocella II, A. J., Drew, C., George, A. E., Ketenci, S., Lupinacci, J., Purdy, I., & Schatz, J. L. (2019). *Education for total liberation: Critical animal pedagogy and teaching against speciesism.* Peter Lang.

Pellow, D. N. (2014). *Total liberation: The power and promise of animal rights and the radical Earth movement.* University of Minnesota Press.

Socha, K. (2012). *Women, destruction, and the avant-garde: A paradigm for animal liberation.* Brill Rodopi.

White, R. J. (2017). Rising to the challenge of capitalism and the commodification of animals: Post-capitalism, anarchist economies and vegan praxis. In D. Nibert (Ed.), *Animal oppression and capitalism.* Praeger.

White, R. J., & Springer, S. (2018). Making space for anarchist geographies in critical animal studies. In J. Sorenson & A. Matuoka (Eds.), *Critical animal studies: Towards trans-species social justice.* Rowman and Littlefield International.

CHAPTER ONE

When the Animal-Industrial Complex Grows … Leaves?

ALLISON GRAY

As a critical interdisciplinary scholar, I find the field of critical animal studies (CAS) very welcoming. The main tenets of CAS include a commitment to comprehensive practice-based efforts which prioritize intersectionality and anti-hierarchical politics (Best et al., 2007; Nocella II et al., 2015). Its overarching goal is total liberation of the Earth and all its human and nonhuman animals, accomplished via social justice movements, constructive collaborations, and radical strategies. In this chapter I connect CAS to a green criminology perspective to critically question the role of plant-meat in the goal of total liberation, conceptualized broadly as the realization and advancement of an ecocentric non-speciesist 'meaty' food product that both limits anthropocentric ecocide and intervenes in violence against 'livestock' animals. In doing so, I explore the complex role of plant-meat in the animal-industrial complex and its potential in mitigating the intersectional harms of the animal agriculture industry.

PLANT-MEAT

The first written record of plant-meat dates to 1301 in China, albeit much older records have been found about tofu around 965 CE. This record was a recipe for mock eel using a base of wheat gluten (Shurtleff & Aoyagi, 2014). Prior to the 20th century, plant-meat products were predominately composed of wheat gluten or nuts. Throughout the 1900s, soy-based plant-meats emerged and became common mid-century, especially using defatted soy protein, better known as texturized vegetable protein (TVP) (Sadler, 2004). During this time and into the 21st century, new technologies emerged that were able to enhance the fibrous structures of plant-meat to mimic animal-based meat's texture (Akdogan, 1999), and recipes often reached this goal by using a combination of ingredients increasingly including peas, chickpeas, rice, maize, fungi, bacteria, and even some attempts with incorporating seaweed (e.g., spirulina) (Grahl et al., 2018). The advancement of the technological means of processing has provided a variety of high-protein ingredients for use in plant-meat products that help to meet human protein and nutritional needs (Kumar et al., 2017).

These previous versions of plant-meat were frequently constrained by issues with texture, flavor, and taste and its need to possess similar sensory attributes of meat (Dekkers et al., 2018). In other words, plant-meat did not succeed at becoming a staple of the global populations because it was not meaty enough. However, unlike the image of gooey bland tofu, today's plant-meat products bleed, sizzle, and taste like 'real meat' thanks to new technologies in processing the soy, peas, wheat, and beans of which they are comprised. For example, Beyond Meat's plant-based beef products are colored with beet juice to give them a similar look to meat, and Impossible Food's plant-based beef products include a vegetarian heme—essentially plant-blood—that gives them a similar (bloody) taste as meat.

Plant-meat can also play a significant role in mitigating the climate catastrophe. 'Livestock' production and meat consumption are leading contributors to anthropogenic greenhouse gas (GHG) emissions (Bailey et al., 2014; Steinfeld et al., 2006), while also threatening ecosystem biodiversity and contributing to species extinction (Emery, 2018; Machovina et al., 2015), and using intensive land practices leading to deforestation, pollution, and jeopardizing fresh water availability (Rizvi et al., 2018; Roser & Ritchie, 2018). To state it simply, 'livestock' farming is killing the planet (Butler & Di Leo, 2019).

Across all diets, animal products with the *lowest* environmental impact exceed the *average* vegetable protein substitute on measures of acidification, eutrophication, land use, and GHG emissions and global warming potential (GWP) (Poore & Nemecek, 2018; Willett et al., 2019). Research shows that GHG emissions associated with 'livestock' production and animal product consumption are only reduced approximately 9% by the application of new, more efficient production technologies, and this potential increases to only 10% in future estimates by 2050, which is significantly less than the potential of plant-based diets reducing emissions by up to 80% (Springmann et al., 2018). This limit of the potential of technology is because there is not sufficient room for change in the biophysical characteristics of 'livestock' animals—they will continue to require (high) levels of water and land (feed) and will produce emissions through enteric fermentation processes (Willett et al., 2019).

On average, plant-meats have very similar carbon footprints, GHG emissions, and land use impact to pulses or beans, regardless of the main ingredient (soy, wheat, nuts, etc.) in which they are comprised (Keoleian & Heller, 2018; Mejia et al., 2019; Ujué et al., 2019). As processed products, plant-meat requires high amounts of energy, but the majority (45%) of energy use and emissions associated with plant-meat production is due to manufacturing processes and running the production facilities (Mejia et al., 2019). Over time with shifts away from carbon-based fuel and power, this segment of the life cycle of plant-meat is expected to decrease.

Plant-meats are figurative and literal replacements for animal-based meats (Adams, 2018). As such, high-protein plant-based food products with long cultural histories and their own identities apart from animal-based meat (e.g., tofu, tempeh) do not fall under the definitional umbrella of plant-meat. Rather, plant-meat is meat without animals—or at least without animals' bodies.

A RE-MEATIFICATION OF DIETS

The average global rate of meat consumption (per year) is currently approximately 42 kilograms per person and projected to increase to over 50 kilograms per person by the year 2050 (FAO, 2017; Johnson & Villumsen, 2018). To put this into perspective, the average national dietary guideline recommends about 50–60 grams of meat daily—a proportion the average global citizen is more than doubling at about 120 grams daily (Godfray et al., 2018). Since the 1950s, the global population has approximately doubled while the average rate of global meat consumption has increased nearly five-fold—labeled the meatification of diets, or the ever-increasing rates of consumption of excessive quantities of meat (continually re-) facilitated through a network of (powerful) political, economic, and agricultural processes (Weis, 2013, 2015).

This shift is not universally experienced. First, there are proportional differences in consumption rates between types of meat. The last decade has witnessed increases in the production and consumption of fish (Kinver, 2016) and poultry (Henchion et al., 2014), with often parallel decreases in red meat consumption. Second, there are regional differences in which countries are experiencing meat consumption rate changes (Weis, 2015). Rising measures of global per capita meat consumption are largely due to the significant increase in meat-eating in so-called developing countries, especially throughout Asia and parts of South America (Godfray et al., 2018; Jakobsen & Hansen, 2020).

Alternatively, accounts of so-called developed countries such as Canada, meat consumption patterns remain relatively stable, although some studies suggest individuals are, on average, eating slightly less meat (The Nielsen Company, 2017; Walton, 2017). This is linked to the growth of a group of individuals identifying as 'flexitarians' who aim to make their diets less meat-intensive, but are not strict vegetarians or vegans (Dagevos & Voordouw, 2013; Raphaely & Marinova, 2016).

From this, some argue we are experiencing the beginning of a global de-meatification of diets where the relative importance of meat consumption is beginning to decline and the world may be passing the age of 'peak meat' (Morris, 2018). However, I argue that this could be understood as the start of a very different dietary transformation, what I am calling a *re-meatification* of diets, characterized by the idea of 'meat' remaining central but it is increasingly composed of plants rather than animals—or, plant-meat.

Between 2013 and 2017, the number of plant-meat products launched across the globe nearly doubled (Mintel, 2018) with estimates that by 2054 alternative protein sources may have 33% of the protein market share (Lux Research Inc., 2014). Multiple organizations and celebrities have thrown trillions of dollars at the concept of meat alternatives (Wiener-Bronner, 2019) and restaurants and fast food eateries (like Burger King and Kentucky Fried Chicken) are racing to introduce plant-meat options for their customers. In Canada, sales of plant-based protein products between 2016 and 2017 grew 7% at $1.5 billion (CDN) (The Nielsen Company, 2017). In the US, plant-based food industry sales grew 20% to $3.3 billion (USD) between 2017 and 2018, compared to 8% growth between 2016 and 2017. However, plant-based *protein* product (re: plant-meat) sales specifically grew 24–30% to $670 million (USD) between 2017 and 2018, compared to 6% growth between 2016 and 2017 (Plant Based Foods Association, 2018; The Nielsen Company, 2018).

These industrial and market changes have impacted consumption. Reports estimate that 43% of Canadians are attempting to incorporate more plant-based proteins in their diets—despite only 6% and 2% of Canadians identifying as vegetarian and vegan, respectively (The Nielsen Company, 2017). More than half of Canadians eat plant-meat (53%), including 18% which consume plant-meat products multiple times per week (Mintel, 2018). Individuals eating plant-based are not identifying with specific vegetarian or vegan diets, but are a growing group of 'flexitarians' (Raphaely & Marinova, 2016) or plant-based dieters (Twine, 2018). That is, everyone—from meat-lovers to vegans—is increasingly consuming plant-meats (Twine, 2018), with Adrian Gastevski, the exclusive distributor of Beyond Meat, reporting that 86% of the consumers who eat their plant-meat products are omnivores (Chiorando, 2018).

The animal agriculture industry has responded to this growth in demand. Food corporations, including leading meat processing companies, have been purchasing plant-meat companies over the last couple decades. In 1999, Kellogg bought Morningstar Farms and later in 2000 Heinz-Kraft bought Boca. More recently, Pinnacle Foods bought Gardein in 2014, Nestlé owns Garden Gourmet and bought Sweet Earth in 2017, Monde Nissin Corporation owns Quorn and Cauldron, and Maple Leaf Foods bought Lightlife and Field Roast in 2017. This concentration of plant-meat manufacturing in the hands of large food corporations is likely to further push plant-meat products into mainstream markets (although this may further corporatize plant-meat and support capitalist endeavors—something CAS is quick to critique). For example, a few years ago Dean Foods, a powerful dairy processor, bought Silk, a plant-milk company. This move ended up being a factor in the success and popularity of plant-milk, which now holds more than 10% of the milk market—a shift which, in theory, should happen in the plant-meat market which holds just over 1% of the meat market currently (Ball, 2017). This is the case of Lightlife products, which rather than relying on venture capital (which Beyond Meat and Impossible Foods do) has the resources of a large corporation, Maple Leaf Foods, to produce, market, and sell it (Shanker, 2019).

In sum, the growth of the plant-meat industry is strongly linked with both market and corporate forces (Goodland & Anhang, 2009) but the speed of its rise is due to significant consumer demand (Nierenberg, 2020), including a significant jump during the COVID-19 pandemic (Bunge & Haddon, 2020; Kart, 2020). Opposed to meat-based protein alternatives—cultured meat, insects, etc.—plant-meat is 'meaty' slab of vegetables and grains, and while it represents dead edible animals, it is plant-based. The re-meatification of diets calls into question the role of plant-meat in mitigating the intersectional harms contributed by animal agriculture against both the natural environment and nonhuman animals. Green criminology can help supplement a CAS perspective concerning the environmental harms of animal-based meat.

GREEN CRIMINOLOGY FOR THE ANIMALS

Green criminology is a branch of critical criminology that directs attention to broader (in)direct harms and crimes involving the environment and (non)human animals (Brisman & South, 2013). While "there is no green criminology theory as such" (White, 2013a, p. 22), green criminology offers a distinct post-human perspective to problematize the social order. More specifically, green criminology is a justice-oriented perspective that broadly recognizes and interprets a variety of context-specific crimes and harms that victimize human animals, nonhuman animals, and the natural environment (often simultaneously)—an approach that overlaps well with the main tenets of CAS. This chapter aims to be one voice (among others: e.g., Taylor & Fitzgerald, 2018) embracing both green criminology and critical animal studies to problematize meat production and consumption as contributing to the abuse of nonhuman animals and environmental harms. To do so requires taking these concepts of ecocentrism, peacemaking, non-speciesism, and (total) liberation and applying them to practice—namely, plant-meat consumption.

Green criminology often includes a social harm approach to its orientation which recognizes and studies social acts and omissions, regardless of intention, that have been historically and commonly excluded from criminological analysis (Tombs, 2018). Broader (traditional) criminology, bound by legal discursive boundaries of 'crime', tends to focus on matters directly involving legal regulations, the criminal justice system, and those directly involved—the police, the courts, and the prisons, as well as (human) offenders, and (human) victims. This narrow focus limits the discipline's contemporary relevance and neglects nonhuman-related issues (Hall et al., 2016). By considering harms alongside illegal behavior, green criminology can facilitate a less distorted view of the world (Hillyard & Tombs, 2004) by extending the criminological gaze to recognize 'lawful but awful' activities (Passas, 2005). Green criminology also prioritizes critical reflection on and evaluation of ontological and epistemological approaches in order to shift away from perpetuating animal/nature,human/culture binaries and privileging human subjectivity and liberty to embracing an inter-relational focus that ideologically and behaviorally re-builds our relationship with other animals and the natural environment (Brisman & South, 2018b; McClanahan, 2019).

To do so, and adhere to the liberation and intersectional goals of critical animal studies (see Nocella II et al., 2014), green criminology must ensure it embraces a nonspeciesist and non-anthropocentric peacemaking standpoint. Peacemaking criminology critically questions the legitimacy of existing socio-cultural, political, and economic arrangements (including how they produce injustice) (Wozniak, 2002), but unfortunately has not been widely embraced in (green) criminology and has only recently been directly named (e.g., McClanahan & Brisman, 2015). Peacemaking requires us "to transcend the barriers that separate us from one another, and to live everyday life with a sense of interdependence" (Quinney, 2000b, p. 26). My focus on integrating peacemaking criminology with green criminology centers on the 'spirit' of peacemaking that entails the (radical) transformation of violent, anthropocentric, and harmful (normative) interactions among humans, nonhuman animals, and the natural environment into caring, compassionate, and ecocentric relationships (McClanahan & Brisman, 2015; Quinney, 2000a).

Within this framework, ecocentrism is an eco-philosophical orientation that responsibilizes humans for upholding the integrity and intrinsic value of other species and the natural environment. In opposition to ecocentrism, anthropocentrism positions humans as morally, mentally, and biologically superior to other species and the natural environment which prioritizes human interests and liberty and allocates others as means for human goals (Brisman & South, 2018a; White, 2018). Ecocentric perspectives fundamentally challenge human exceptionalism, by stressing the inextricable integration and patterns of interaction of humans with other species and the natural environment and ensuring that other living entities' value is not reducible to human instrumental use. Thus, ecocentrism recognizes humans as both destroyers and protectors who are capable of reacting to (and mitigating) their own and others' suffering (Brisman & South, 2018a; White, 2013b)—and in this case, capable of peacemaking.

The nonspeciesist element has experienced less success in green criminology. There exists a notable contingent of researchers who are working towards effective attention to nonhuman species and other beings, including de-commodifying animals and problematizing the (ab)use of 'livestock' and wild animals (Fitzgerald & Tourangeau, 2018; Laestadius, Deckers, & Baran, 2018). Unfortunately, these examples aside, many argue green criminology is failing to embrace a nonspeciesist stance effectively (Sollund, 2013; Taylor & Fitzgerald, 2018). This exemplifies the need for using a CAS perspective to supplement green criminology to ensure it continues working toward nonspeciesist goals. The remainder of the chapter discusses how plant-meat fits into the animal-industrial complex and explores it as a complex struggle in the movement for total liberation.

THE ANIMAL-INDUSTRIAL COMPLEX AND THE MEAT PARADOX

The animal-industrial complex encompasses a multidimensional network of "an extensive range of practices, technologies, images, identities and markets" (Twine, 2012, p. 23) that work to objectify and commodify nonhuman animals "embedded in a capitalist fabric" (Noske, 1989, p. 22). It cumulates into a ubiquitous force that works to enable and celebrate the institutionalized exploitation of nonhuman animals (Salter et al., 2014). Richard Twine (2013) correctly notes the complex includes two inseparable dimensions involving considerations of materiality and semiotics. While the complex cannot be reduced to agricultural or food-related realms, that is my focus here, and I will outline these two dimensions within the meat and plant-meat sectors.

The first dimension of the animal-industrial complex is the physical-material dimension linked with industrial production practices, of which the meatification of diets is a significant component. Meatification is shaped by powerful actors seeking to supply ever greater volumes of (cheap) meat, which gets people to eat more meat, and reap rising profits from this growth. It is driven by the grain-oilseed-livestock complex—or the prioritization (and subsidizing) vast landscapes of monoculture crops to (inefficiently) feed exploding populations of 'livestock' animals (Sans & Combris, 2015; Weis, 2015). In essence, the animal agricultural industry creates a large supply of meat products as cheap as possible to ensure consumption rates remain high and keep growing.

Such low-cost high-output outcomes occur through concentrated animal feeding operations (CAFOs) commonly known as factory farms. These key facilities within the infrastructure of industrial animal agriculture for most of its history have been, and continue to be, invisible—out of sight, out of mind (Ogle, 2013). Humans are further removed from farms, with dwindling farming populations left to produce ever-increasing amounts of sustenance for growing urban populations—a phenomenon termed 'extinction of experience' that is an indirect and direct cause of global environmental degradation and poorer treatment of 'livestock' (Fitzgerald, 2015; Soga & Gaston, 2016). 'Livestock' animals are locked within windowless barns and slaughtering facilities are moved further from urban spaces. Further, multiple regions have even adopted criminal policies banning individuals from taking and/or sharing pictures or videos of the ongoings inside agricultural facilities and/or property (Simon, 2013).

These processes have facilitated the construction of a food rift, or a distancing between humans and food systems and products (Worthy, 2013). In today's globally connected world, food travels thousands of kilometers before it reaches a plate, and details as to its origin, who produces it, how it is processed, and its social and environmental implications are either unknown or reduced to small labels on grocery store shelves or nutrition facts and barcodes all-but-hidden on product packaging—which means the typical consumer has seemingly little knowledge of and control over global food production and systems (Clapp, 2018; Weis, 2007).

This disconnect is particularly experienced in regards to industrial animal agriculture. Beginning with domestication, the relationship between humans and animals has fundamentally changed into the hyper-industrialized, intensified, and commoditized state today where animals are used for profit which (re-) constructs their subordination, objectification, and oppression (Fitzgerald, 2015; Nibert, 2013). This has included a reliance on machinery, science, and technologies which elongates the food chain and distances humans from both ('livestock') animals and the natural environment: "while animal flesh, milk and eggs are being consumed in ever-greater volumes, farm animals are vanishing into environments of concrete and steel, connected through complex and opaque long-distance flows to an increasingly urban world" (Weis, 2016, p. 12). Such 'development' is normalized by these ideological roots of animals-as-commodities that maintains the disconnection and limits questioning of its processes and its animal welfare and socio-ecological implications (Fitzgerald, 2015; Weis, 2013).

The food rift is experienced not just physically but also psychologically (Clapp, 2016; Worthy, 2013) and this is linked with the second dimension of the animal-industrial complex—the discursive-semiotic dimension. Global food culture naturalizes and normalizes eating animals as not just acceptable but necessary and often 'nice' (Chiles & Fitzgerald, 2018). This belief is (incorrectly) presented as inevitable—industrial agriculture must produce this way and consumers must eat this way (Arcari, 2017). Melanie Joy (2011) has termed this ideology as 'carnism,' which, while culturally relevant, classifies some animals as edible but not others, including some cultures (e.g., North American) which support a belief system that considers meat-eating an entitlement (Ogle, 2013). This creates a particularly heavy veil distancing humans' conceptualization of meat as a food commodity from its animal being (Weis, 2013), which represents a 'second death' for 'livestock' animals (Cronon, 1992) as nonhuman animals become absent referents to meat products—that is, animals are separated from their dead bodies and the practice of meat-eating (Adams, 2010).

Turning a blind eye to meat's animalistic characteristics is not just the case of individual decisions, but is institutionalized through social practices. Various forms of media, including children's books and films as well as news media sources, discursively work to distance inedible animals from edible animals, normalizing meat culture (Chiles, 2017). The socialization of meat eating is evidenced in mothers seeking to protect their children from the violence of eating animals and the harshness of the industrial 'livestock' industry through deliberate attempts to shield children from understanding how meat gets on the plate (Cairns & Johnston, 2018). The institutionalized understanding of (some) nonhuman animals as food is problematic and "requires us to consider long-term and foundational issues, and it challenges some of our most deeply held values and beliefs" (Fischer et al., 2007, p. 623).

By obscuring the animality of meat, patterns of high rates of meat consumption are maintained through various belief adaptations, coping strategies, or strategic ignorance (Graça, Calheiros, & Oliveira, 2016). This often results in cognitive dissonance among people who both 'love' yet eat animals or who like meat but dislike harming animals (Kunst & Palacios Haugestad, 2018). This conflict between animal suffering and the practice of meat eating is called the meat paradox (Buttlar & Walther, 2019). The meat paradox involves a repression of the separation between what is animal and what is food (meat), including a moral disengagement that denies animals concern for their suffering (Ang, Chan, & Singh, 2019). This is evidenced when individuals are less empathetic (and feel less disgust) to the slaughtering of animals when presented with processed (e.g., ground) meat compared with versions of meat in animal form, such as a full-roasted pig or fried fish (Kunst & Hohle, 2016). Consumers actively engage in various cognitive strategies, such as denial, repression, and dissociation, to limit their experience of the meat paradox (Dowsett et al., 2018; Kunst & Hohle, 2016).

VEGANIZING THE ANIMAL-INDUSTRIAL COMPLEX?

The concept of plant-meat itself offers a sort of contradiction. Is it plants? Is it meat? Can it be both? Some contend that plant-meat has unexpected merits due to meat's special (socio-cultural) characteristics (Fiddes, 2004). For example, contemporary plant-based burgers (e.g., the Beyond Burger) embrace meat-like features because they were strategically created to entice meat-eaters to change their diet choices (Adams, 2018). Some of the larger plant-meat companies even require grocery stores to stock their products beside their animal-based equivalents in the meat aisle. Many products directly connect with—or, as Twine (2018) argues, intentionally mock—their animal-based counterparts through their naming, but with an added prefix: *tofu*rky, *veggie* burger, *no*-chicken broth, etc. The addition of such modifiers is critiqued for maintaining the division between nature (plants) and animals. Wolpa (2016, p. 90) argues that "meat without animals is an oxymoron only in so far as it is made that way by our own dominant ideologies" and we need to (re-)understand meat as before the signifier. The CEO of Beyond Meat strongly agrees and dislikes the 'fake' modifier because, as a concept, meat is a *true* absent referent, comprised of a combination of elements such as amino acids, proteins, carbs, etc. As such, 'meat' is not predestined to represent animal flesh.

There are also arguments that plant-meat perpetuates the (ab)use of animals as food. Sinclair (2016) argues that plant-meats are never actually free of the animals they intend to substitute—rather, plant-meat reproduces the frameworks which keep animals edible even if they are not eaten directly. She claims that the understanding and pleasure of plant-meats *relies* on their association with and edibility of 'real' meats; plant-meat "still imposes a certain violence on other edible bodies" (Sinclair, 2016, p. 238). While Adams disagrees with Sinclair (Adams, 2016; Adams & Messina, 2018), arguing instead that plant-meat is a form of resistance, she has elsewhere (Adams, 2010) argued that plant-meat is symbolic of the dominance of humanity over animals and enables the extension of this control to plants. Indeed, plant-meat may reinforce Western-centric ideals of eating patterns involving conventional animal foods (Sexton, 2018).

Is plant-meat an impediment to the liberation of animals? No. Unlike in-vitro and/or cultured meat technologies which continue to rely on confining and (ab)using animals and their bodily parts (e.g., muscle tissue cells, fetal growth serum) (Poirier & Russell, 2019), plant-meat is free of animal products in the material sense. Comprised of legumes, beans, pulses, oils, vegetables, herbs and spices, plant-meat products are meaty versions of plants. One objective of critical animal studies is to make animals reappear and rematerialize from the capitalist forces that make animals absent and fragmented (Adams, 2010; Twine, 2012)—a goal that plant-meat can facilitate by physically removing nonhuman animals' bodies from meat products. This shifts human-animal relationships away from that defined via the violent (ab)use and murdering of 'livestock' animals—a change which may be reflected in human-animal relationships outside of the agricultural and consumption realms (e.g., de Backer & Hudders, 2015). For example, individuals with higher plant-meat consumption are significantly more likely to defend the intrinsic value and worth of non-livestock (e.g., 'pets') animals (Gray, 2020).

On the discursive side, the ability of plant-meat in freeing nonhuman animals from conceptualizations of meat and edibility may be subject to greater resistance, in line with Sinclair's (2016) argument. It is a logical expectation, in the shorter term, that the simple cultural habit of defining meat (solely) as animal-based protein would transfer to plant-based versions and thus all 'meat' may normalize the edibility of its plant and animal components. However, this argument relies on a stagnant notion of cultural conceptualization that does not problematize humanity's role. That is, how we define meat is a *human* problem. In the longer term, and with greater availability and accessibility to plant-meat, the concept of meat can be separated from any association with animality and liberate 'livestock' animals from their murderous path to humans' plates. Rather than normalizing the edibility of nonhuman animals, plant-meat would work to normalize the edibility of protein.

The role of plant-meat in total liberation efforts is somewhat more complex. Total liberation is a cultural force working to reveal and intervene in systems of hierarchy, involving both human and nonhuman animals and the natural environment, that "constitute[s] a threat to the core operating principles and assumptions behind the current social order" (Nocella II et al., 2015, p. 3). At first glance, the consumption of plant-meat, particularly to replace animal-based meat, is a threat to current industrial animal agriculture and its excessive meat production and consumption agenda. If you have ever told someone they can no longer eat animal-based meat, I am sure you have experienced backlash exemplifying the institutionalized effect that such meat-eating has on people. Likewise, if you are to tell someone that you eat plant-meat instead of animal-based meat, you would likely also experience criticism for disregarding the normal function of human consumption practices. Not eating animal-based meat itself is a threat to the harmful social order and eating plant-meat can be part of this interference.

Nonetheless, there are ways that plant-meat does not necessarily represent the energy of total liberation. Some concerns, for example, include the potential of extending monoculture agriculture for some plant species to channel inputs (negatively impacting the natural environment) into a growing plant-meat industry, or even the obscuration of human laborer crimes and harms involved in plant-meat fields and manufacturing facilities. These relate to a more significant apprehension about the continuation, and even celebration, of capitalist markets.

Many plant-meat products are owned by corporations within the animal agricultural industry—some of which are country's largest animal-based meat processors (e.g., Maple Leaf Foods in Canada branding their plant-meat as Lightlife). In these cases, the purchase and/or consumption of these plant-meat products become profit for businesses which murder countless animals and promote a carnist ideology. Similarly, plant-meat products from companies with criminal and unethical histories, such as Nestlé with its deforestation, water mining, and formula milk promotion among other problematic labor practices (Chiorando, 2020), question the role of (this form of) plant-meat in mitigating oppressive practices. This is not the case with all plant-meat products, ranging from Turtle Island Food Inc.'s Tofurky brand products which are approved by The Vegan Society in the United Kingdom (The Vegan Society, 2020), and products from local businesses which adhere to ethical guidelines for ingredients and pay laborers living wages (Coven, 2020; The Herbivorous Butcher, 2020).

As a commodity, plant-meat's role in working toward (total) liberation is somewhat limited to the market realm. Through consumerist behavior, individuals are held responsible to be 'good eaters' which does not always and/or sufficiently oppose the violence associated with broader systematic networks of oppression (Lukacs, 2017; Sexton, 2018). Nonetheless, the realm of the consumer is ever-increasingly a significant, unprecedented, and even preferred space for political action, especially regarding social justice matters (Arnould, 2007; Guthman, 2008). I agree with many others who point to the harm in focusing on such binary language (re: citizen-consumer)—which is artificial and abstract, obscures the possibilities of change, and harms the potential for social change (DuPuis & Goodman, 2005; Johnston & Cairns, 2012)—and advocate for a broader understanding of the role of consumption in food politics and social movements.

The reality is that plant-meat has the potential to fulfill a significant and effective role in liberation efforts. The consumption of plant-meat is not the sole solution or the silver bullet, but it could be part of the process. Plant-meat consumption, as a form of consumer-activism, can facilitate a high quantity and frequency of engagement (that is, many individuals can simultaneously participate) (Arnould, 2007; Gray, 2017) while achieving high levels of acceptance and facilitating higher demand for less-oppressive products (Twine, 2018; van der Weele et al., 2019). Of course, change via consumer choice will be most effective in an economic system providing (sustainable) options for everyone not just an affluent few (Lukacs, 2017), and the current and near-future plant-meat market works towards this as it continues to expand access and make its products more affordable.

CONCLUSION

This chapter critically questioned how plant-meat fits into CAS's goal of total liberation. By bringing in key lessons from green criminology and utilizing the concept of the animal-industrial complex, I argue that plant-meat does have a promising role in liberation struggles, but its potential effectiveness is complicated. Plant-meat, as a food category, cannot be blanketed as a perfect solution across claims for social justice, ecocentrism, or anti-speciesism. Certain brands, certain ingredients, and the corporations manufacturing the products matter, as is the case with many food products. However, plant-meat is progress.

Plant-meat rejects the carnist idea that nonhuman animals' lives are lesser than humans' lives by symbolically removing the edible characterization from nonhuman animals and by literally removing their flesh from food. Consuming anything, including food, is one point along a complex and long chain of processes across space and time where "to consume an object [or being] ... is to validate its harmful history and instigate its harmful future" (O'Brien, 2008, p. 10). The opposite is also true, where consuming something (else) can endorse peacemaking relationships with others and liberate the oppressed—a possibility for the role of plant-meat within an unsustainable and violent world.

REFERENCES

Adams, C. J. (2010). *The sexual politics of meat: A feminist-vegetarian critical theory* (20th anniversary ed.). Bloomsbury Academic.

Adams, C. J. (2016). Ethical spectacles and seitan-making: Beyond the sexual politics of meat – A response to Sinclair. In B. Donaldson & C. Carter (Eds.), *The future of meat without animals* (pp. 249–256). Rowman & Littlefield International.

Adams, C. J. (2018). *Burger.* Bloomsbury Academic.

Adams, C. J., & Messina, V. (2018). *Protest kitchen: Fight injustice, save the planet, and fuel your resistance one meal at a time.* Conari Press.

Akdogan, H. (1999). High moisture food extrusion. *International journal of food science & technology, 34*(3), 195-20.

Ang, C. S., Chan, N. N., & Singh, L. (2019). A comparison study of meat eaters and non-meat eaters on mind attribution and moral disengagement of animals. *Appetite, 136*, 80–85.

Arcari, P. (2017). Normalised, human-centric discourses of meat and animals in climate change, sustainability and food security literature. *Journal of the Agriculture, Food, and Human Values Society, 34*(1), 69–86.

Arnould, E. J. (2007). Should consumer citizens escape the market? *The Annals of the American Academy of Political and Social Science, 611*(1), 96–111.

Bailey, R., Froggatt, A., & Wellesley, L. (2014). *Livestock–climate change's forgotten sector: Global public opinion on meat and dairy consumption.* Chatham House.

Ball, M. (2017, December). *Transforming the meat industry from the inside out*. Good Food Institute. https://www.gfi.org/transforming-the-meat-industry-from-the-inside

Best, S., Nocella II, A. J., Kahn, R., Gigliotti, C., & Kemmerer, L. (2007). *Introducing critical animal studies*. Institute for Critical Animal Studies. http://www.criticalanimalstudies.org/wp-content/uploads/2009/09/Introducing-Critical-Animal-Studies-2007.pdf

Brisman, A., & South, N. (2013). Introduction: Horizons, issues and relationships in green criminology. In N. South & A. Brisman (Eds.), *Routledge international handbook of Green criminology* (pp. 1–23). New York: Routledge.

Brisman, A., & South, N. (2018a). Green criminology and environmental crimes and harms. *Sociology Compass*, e12650.

Brisman, A., & South, N. (2018b). Green criminology, zemiology, and comparative and inter-relational justice in the Anthropocene era. In A. Boukli & J. Kotzé (Eds.), *Zemiology: Reconnecting crime and social harm* (pp. 203–221). Palgrave Macmillan.

Bunge, J., & Haddon, H. (2020, May). Coronavirus meat shortages have plant-based food makers' mouths watering. *The Wall Street Journal*. https://www.wsj.com/articles/coronavirus-meat-shortages-have-plant-based-food-makers-mouths-watering-11589371206

Butler, J., & Di Leo, J. (20219). Envirocidal: How livestock farming is killing the planet. *Viva!* https://cdn.viva.org.uk/wp-content/uploads/2020/03/ENVIROCIDAL_MAY_2019.pdf

Buttlar, B., & Walther, E. (2019). Dealing with the meat paradox: Threat leads to moral disengagement from meat consumption. *Appetite, 137*, 73–80.

Cairns, K., & Johnston, J. (2018). On (not) knowing where your food comes from: Meat, mothering and ethical eating. *Agriculture and Human Values, 35*(3), 569–580.

Chiles, R. M. (2017). Hidden in plain sight: How industry, mass media, and consumers' everyday habits suppress food controversies. *Sociologia Ruralis, 57*(S1), 791–815.

Chiles, R. M., & Fitzgerald, A. (2018). Why is meat so important in Western history and culture? A genealogical critique of biophysical and political-economic explanations. *Journal of the Agriculture, Food, and Human Values Society, 35*(1), 1–17.

Chiorando, M. (2018, November). 86% of consumers of vegan meat products are meat eaters. *Plant Based News*. https://plantbasednews.org/lifestyle/86-consumers-vegan-beyond-meat-meat-eaters/

Chiorando, M. (2020, September). Nestlé brings plant-based bacon cheeseburger to foodservice sector. *Plant Based News*. https://plantbasednews.org/lifestyle/nestle-plant-based-bacon-cheeseburger-foodservice/

Clapp, J. (2016). *Food* (2nd ed.). Polity Press.

Clapp, J. (2018). Mega-mergers on the menu: Corporate concentration and the politics of sustainability in the global food system. *Global Environmental Politics, 18*(2), 12–33.

Coven. (2020). Coven Market. http://covenmarket.com/

Cronon, W. (1992). *Nature's metropolis: Chicago and the Great West*. W.W. Norton & Company Inc.

Dagevos, H., & Voordouw, J. (2013). Sustainability and meat consumption: Is reduction realistic? *Sustainability: Science, Practice, & Policy, 9*(2), 60–69.

De Backer, C. J. S., & Hudders, L. (2015). Meat morals: Relationship between meat consumption consumer attitudes towards human and animal welfare and moral behavior. *Meat Science, 99*, 68–74.

Dekkers, B. L., Boom, R. M., & van Der Goot, A. J. (2018). Structuring processes for meat analogues. *Trends in Food Science & Technology, 81*, 25–36.

Dowsett, E., Semmler, C., Bray, H., Ankeny, R. A., & Chur-Hansen, A. (2018). Neutralising the meat paradox: Cognitive dissonance, gender, and eating animals. *Appetite, 123*, 280–288.

DuPuis, E. M., & Goodman, D. (2005). Should we go 'home' to eat?: Toward a reflexive politics of localism. *Journal of Rural Studies, 21*(3), 359–371.

Emery, I. (2018). Meat's sustainability problem. *The Good Food Institute.* https://www.gfi.org/images/uploads/2018/10/AnimalAgEnvironment.pdf

FAO. (2017). The future of food and agriculture: Trends and challenges. *United Nations.* http://www.fao.org/3/a-i6583e.pdf.

Fiddes, N. (2004). *Meat a natural symbol.* Taylor and Francis.

Fischer, J., Manning, A. D., Steffen, W., Rose, D. B., Daniell, K., Felton, A., ... Wade, A. (2007). Mind the sustainability gap. *Trends in Ecology & Evolution, 22*(12), 621–624.

Fitzgerald, A. J. (2015). *Animals as food: (Re)connecting production, processing, consumption, and impacts.* Michigan State University Press.

Fitzgerald, A. J., & Tourangeau, W. (2018). Crime versus harm in the transportation of animals: A closer look at Ontario's 'pig trial'. In A. Gray & R. Hinch (Eds.), *A handbook of food crime: Immoral and illegal practices in the food industry and what to do about them* (pp. 213–228). Policy Press.

Godfray, H. C. J., Aveyard, P., Garnett, T., Hall, J. W., Key, T. J., Lorimer, J., ... Jebb, S. A. (2018). Meat consumption, health, and the environment. *Science, 361*(6399), 1–8.

Goodland, R., & Anhang, J. (2009). Livestock and climate change: What if the key actors in climate change are... cows, pigs, and chickens? *World Watch Institute.* http://www.worldwatch.org/files/pdf/Livestock%20and%20Climate%20Change.pdf

Graça, J., Calheiros, M. M., & Oliveira, A. (2016). Situating moral disengagement: Motivated reasoning in meat consumption and substitution. *Personality and Individual Differences, 90*, 353–364.

Grahl, S., Palanisamy, M., Strack, M., Meier-Dinkel, L., Toepfl, S., & MöRlein, D. (2018). Towards more sustainable meat alternatives: How technical parameters affect the sensory properties of extrusion products derived from soy and algae. *Journal of Cleaner Production, 198*, 962–971.

Gray, A. (2017). Dueling the consumer-activist dualism: The consumption experiences of modern food activists. *Future of Food, 5*(3), 35–45.

Gray, A. (2020). *Eating in the Anthropocene: Perceptions of dietary-based environmental harm and the role of plant-meat consumption.* (Doctor of Philosophy). University of Windsor.

Guthman, J. (2008). Neoliberalism and the making of food politics in California. *Geoforum, 39*(3), 1171–1183.

Hall, M., Maher, J., Nurse, A., Potter, G., South, N., & Wyatt, T. (Eds.). (2016). *Green criminology in the 21st century: Contemporary debates and future directions in the study of environmental harm.* Routledge.

Henchion, M., McCarthy, M., Resconi, V. C., & Troy, D. (2014). Meat consumption: Trends and quality matters. *Meat Science, 98*(3), 561–568.

Hillyard, P., & Tombs, S. (2004). *Beyond criminology: Taking harm seriously.* Pluto Press.

Jakobsen, J., & Hansen, A. (2020). Geographies of meatification: An emerging Asian meat complex. *Globalizations, 17*(1), 1–17.

Johnson, B., & Villumsen, G. (2018). Environmental aspects of natural resource intensive development: The case of agriculture. *Innovation and Development, 8*(1), 167–188.

Johnston, J., & Cairns, K. (2012). Eating for change. In R. Mukherjee & S. Banet-Weiser (Eds.), *Commodity activism: Cultural resistance in neoliberal times* (Vol. 219–239). New York University Press.

Joy, M. (2011). *Why we love dogs, eat pigs, and wear cows.* Conari Press.

Kart, J. (2020, July). People buying more alternative meat, expected to consume less real meat through 2025. *Forbes.* https://www.forbes.com/sites/jeffkart/2020/07/17/people-buying-more-alternative-meat-expected-to-consume-less-real-meat-through-2025/#6e60fc901a06

Keoleian, G. A., & Heller, M. C. (2018, September). Beyond meat's beyond burger life cycle assessment: A detailed comparison between a plant-based and an animal-based protein source. *University of Michigan.* http://css.umich.edu/sites/default/files/publication/CSS18-10.pdf

Kinver, M. (2016, July). UN: Global fish consumption per capita hits record high. *BBC News.* http://www.bbc.com/news/science-environment-36716579

Kumar, P., Chatli, M. K., Mehta, N., Singh, P., Malav, O. P., & Verma, A. K. (2017). Meat analogues: Health promising sustainable meat substitutes. *Critical Reviews in Food Science and Nutrition, 57*(5), 923–932.

Kunst, J. R., & Hohle, S. M. (2016). Meat eaters by dissociation: How we present, prepare and talk about meat increases willingness to eat meat by reducing empathy and disgust. *Appetite, 105,* 758–774.

Kunst, J. R., & Palacios Haugestad, C. A. (2018). The effects of dissociation on willingness to eat meat are moderated by exposure to unprocessed meat: A cross-cultural demonstration. *Appetite, 120,* 356–366.

Laestadius, L. I., Deckers, J., & Baran, S. (2018). Food crimes, harms and carnist technologies. In A. Gray & R. Hinch (Eds.), *A handbook of food crime: Immoral and illegal practices in the food industry and what to do about them* (pp. 295–312). Policy Press.

Lukacs, M. (2017, July). Neoliberalism has conned us into fighting climate change as individuals. *The Guardian.* https://www.theguardian.com/environment/true-north/2017/jul/17/neoliberalism-has-conned-us-into-fighting-climate-change-as-individuals

Lux Research Inc. (2014, December). WhoPea: Plant sources are changing the protein landscape. *State of the Market Report.* https://members.luxresearchinc.com/research/report/16091

Machovina, B., Feeley, K. J., & Ripple, W. J. (2015). Biodiversity conservation: The key is reducing meat consumption. *Science of the Total Environment, 536,* 419–431.

McClanahan, B. (2019). Earth–world–planet: Rural ecologies of horror and dark green criminology. *Theoretical Criminology 24*(4), 633–650.

McClanahan, B., & Brisman, A. (2015). Climate change and peacemaking criminology: Ecophilosophy, peace and security in the 'war on climate change'. *The Official Journal of the ASC Division on Critical Criminology and the ACJS Section on Critical Criminology, 23*(4), 417–431.

Mejia, M. A., Fresán, U., Harwatt, H., Oda, K., Uriegas-Mejia, G., & Sabaté, J. (2019). Life cycle assessment of the production of a large variety of meat nalogs by three diverse factories. *Journal of Hunger & Environmental Nutrition, 15*(5), 1–13.

Mintel. (2018, April). Positive future for plant proteins: More than half of Canadians eat meat alternatives. *Mintel.* http://www.mintel.com/press-centre/food-and-drink/positive-future-for-plant-proteins-more-than-half-of-canadians-eat-meat-alternatives

Morris, C. (2018). 'Taking the politics out of broccoli': Debating (de)meatification in UK national and regional newspaper coverage of the Meat Free Mondays campaign. *Sociologia Ruralis, 58*(2), 433–452.

Nibert, D. A. (2013). *Animal oppression & human violence: Domesecration, capitalism, and global conflict*. Columbia University Press.

Nierenberg, A. (2020, May). Plant-based 'meats' catch on in the pandemic. *The New York Times*. https://www.nytimes.com/2020/05/22/dining/plant-based-meats-coronavirus.html

Nocella II, A. J., Sorenson, J., Socha, K., & Matsuoka, A. (Eds.). (2014). *Defining critical animal studies: An intersectional social justice approach for liberation*. Peter Lang Inc.

Nocella II, A. J., White, R. J., & Cudworth, E. (Eds.). (2015). *Anarchism and animal liberation: Essays on complementary elements of total liberation*. McFarland & Company Inc.

Noske, B. (1989). *Human and other animals*. Pluto Press.

O'Brien, M. (2008). Criminal degradations of consumer culture. In R. Sollund (Ed.), *Global harms: Ecological crime and speciesism*. Nova Science.

Ogle, M. (2013). *In meat we trust: An unexpected history of carnivore America*. Houghton Mifflin Harcourt Publishing Company.

Passas, N. (2005). Lawful but awful: 'Legal corporate crimes'. *The Journal of Socio-Economics, 34*(6), 771–786.

Plant Based Foods Association. (2018). Plant-based food sales grow 20 percent: New Nielsen retail data commission by the Plant Based Foods Association shows plant-based alternatives outpacing overall food sales by 10X. *PBFA*. https://plantbasedfoods.org/consumer-access/nielsen-data-release-2018/

Poirier, N., & Russell, J. (2019). Does in vitro meat constitute animal liberation? *Journal of Animal Ethics, 9*(2), 199–211.

Poore, J., & Nemecek, T. (2018). Reducing food's environmental impacts through producers and consumers. *Science, 360*(6392), 987–992.

Quinney, R. (2000a). *Bearing witness to crime and social justice*. SUNY Press.

Quinney, R. (2000b). Socialist humanism and the problem of crime: Thinking about Erich Fromm in the development of critical/peacemaking criminology. In K. Anderson & R. Quinney (Eds.), *Erich Fromm and critical criminology: Beyond the punitive society* (pp. 21–30). University of Illinois Press.

Raphaely, T., & Marinova, D. (Eds.). (2016). *Impact of meat consumption on health and environmental sustainability*. IGI Global.

Rizvi, S., Pagnutti, C., Fraser, E., Bauch, C. T., & Anand, M. (2018). Global land use implications of dietary trends. *PLoS ONE, 13*(8), e0200781.

Roser, M., & Ritchie, H. (2018). Yields and land use in agriculture. *Our World in Data*. https://ourworldindata.org/yields-and-land-use-in-agriculture

Sadler, M. J. (2004). Meat alternatives—market developments and health benefits. *Trends in Food Science & Technology, 15*(5), 250–260.

Salter, C., Nocella II, A. J., & Bentley, J. K. C. (Eds.). (2014). *Animals and war: Confronting the military-animal industrial complex*. Rowman & Littlefield.

Sans, P., & Combris, P. (2015). World meat consumption patterns: An overview of the last fifty years (1961–2011). *Meat Science, 109*, 106–111.

Sexton, A. E. (2018). Eating for the post-Anthropocene: Alternative proteins and the biopolitics of edibility. *Transactions of the Institute of British Geographers, 43*(4), 586–600.

Shanker, D. (2019, January). Maple Leaf has high hopes for plant-based burger. *The Star*. https://financialpost.com/news/retail-marketing/canadian-meat-giant-maple-leaf-debuts-new-plant-based-burger

Shurtleff, W., & Aoyagi, A. (2014). *History of meat alternatives (965 CE to 2014): Extensively annotated bibliography and sourcebook.* Soyinfo Center.

Simon, D. R. (2013). *Meatonomics: How the rigged economics of meat and dairy make you consume too much.* Conari Press.

Sinclair, R. (2016). The sexual politics of meatless meat: (In)edible others and the myth of flesh without sacrifice. In B. Donaldson & C. Carter (Eds.), *The future of meat without animals* (pp. 229–248). Rowman & Littlefield International.

Soga, M., & Gaston, K. J. (2016). Extinction of experience: The loss of human–nature interactions. *Frontiers in Ecology and the Environment, 14*(2), 94–101.

Sollund, R. (2013). Animal trafficking and trade: Abuse and species injustice. In R. Walters, D. Westerhuis, & T. Wyatt (Eds.), *Emerging issues in green criminology* (pp. 72–92). Palgrave Macmillan.

Springmann, M., Clark, M., Mason-D'croz, D., Wiebe, K., Bodirsky, B. L., Lassaletta, L., ... Willett, W. (2018). Options for keeping the food system within environmental limits. *Nature, 562*(7728), 519–525.

Steinfeld, H., Gerber, P., Wassenaar, T., Castel, V., Rosales, M., & de Haan, C. (2006). Livestock's long shadow: Environmental issues and options. *FAO.* http://www.fao.org/3/a0701e/a0701e.pdf

Taylor, N., & Fitzgerald, A. (2018). Understanding animal (ab)use: Green criminological contributions, missed opportunities and a way forward. *Theoretical Criminology, 22*(3), 402–425.

The Herbivorous Butcher. (2020). The Herbivorous Butcher. www.theherbivorousbutcher.com

The Nielsen Company. (2017, September). Plant-based proteins are gaining dollar share among North Americans. *The Nielsen Company.* https://www.nielsen.com/ca/en/insights/news/2017/plant-based-proteins-are-gaining-dollar-share-among-north-americans.html

The Nielsen Company. (2018, June). Plant-based food options are sprouting growth for retailers. *The Nielson Company.* https://www.nielsen.com/us/en/insights/news/2018/plant-based-food-options-are-sprouting-growth-for-retailers.html

The Vegan Society. (2020). Trademarked Products. https://www.vegansociety.com/search/products/t

Tombs, S. (2018). For pragmatism and politics: Crime, social harm and zemiology. In A. Boukli & J. Kotzé (Eds.), *Zemiology: Reconnecting crime and social harm* (pp. 11–31). Macmillan.

Twine, R. (2012). Revealing the 'Animal-Industrial Complex' – A concept and methods for critical animal studies? *Journal for Critical Animal Studies, 10*(1), 12–39.

Twine, R. (2013). Addressing the animal-industrial complex. In R. Corbey & A. Lanjouw (Eds.), *The politics of species: Reshaping our relationships with other animals.* Cambridge University Press.

Twine, R. (2018). Materially constituting a sustainable food transition: The case of vegan eating practice. *Sociology, 52*(1), 166–181.

Ujué, F., Maximino Alfredo, M., Winston, J. C., Karen, J.-S., & Joan, S. (2019). Meat analogs from different protein sources: A comparison of their sustainability and nutritional content. *Sustainability, 11*(12), 3231.

van Der Weele, C., Feindt, P., Jan van Der Goot, A., van Mierlo, B., & van Boekel, M. (2019). Meat alternatives: An integrative comparison. *Trends in Food Science & Technology, 88*, 505–512.

Walton, S. (2017). *The plant-based diet evolution: The consumer, scientific evidence, and food formulation.* New Orleans, LA: The Institute of Food Technologists: Feed your future.

Weis, T. (2007). *The global food economy: The battle for the future of farming.* Palgrave Macmillan.

Weis, T. (2013). *The ecological hoofprint: The global burden of industrial livestock*. Zed Books.

Weis, T. (2015). Meatification and the madness of the doubling narrative. *Canadian Food Studies, 2*(2), 296–303.

Weis, T. (2016). Towards 120 billion: Dietary change and animal lives. *Radical Philosophy, 199*(5), 8–13.

White, R. (2013a). Eco-global criminology and the political economy of environmental harm. In N. South & A. Brisman (Eds.), *Routledge international handbook of green criminology* (pp. 243–260). Routledge.

White, R. (2013b). *Environmental harm: An eco-justice perspective*. Policy Press.

White, R. (2018). Ecocentrism and criminal justice. *Theoretical Criminology, 22*(3), 342–362.

Wiener-Bronner, D. (2019, May). Serena Williams, Jay-Z and Katy Perry are investing in Impossible Foods. *CNN*. https://www.cnn.com/2019/05/13/investing/impossible-foods-investment-serena-williams-jay-z/index.html

Willett, W., Rockström, J., Loken, B., Springmann, M., Lang, T., Vermeulen, S., ... Murray, C. J. L. (2019). Food in the Anthropocene: The EAT– Lancet Commission on healthy diets from sustainable food systems. *The Lancet, 393*(10170), 447–492.

Wolpa, A. (2016). Seeing meat without animals: Attitudes for the future. In B. Donaldson & C. Carter (Eds.), *The future of meat without animals* (pp. 87–96). Rowman & Littlefield International.

Worthy, K. (2013). *Invisible nature: Healing the destructive divide between people and the environment*. Prometheus Books.

Wozniak, J. F. (2002). Toward a theoretical model of peacemaking criminology: An essay in honor of Richard Quinney. *Crime & Delinquency, 48*(2), 204–231.

CHAPTER TWO

Agency and Suffering in Animal Studies and in Animal Liberation

MARYLINE EL KHOURY AND KENZO JACQUEMIN

The issues of animal agency and animal suffering are approached differently depending on whether it is in the field of animal studies or radical political activism, including critical animal studies. To be clear when we use the term "animal studies" we do not refer to the field grounded in the medical-industrial complex that aims to test on animals and perform vivisection, although this is where the term originated. Instead, we refer to a field of study that converges human and social sciences as well as other disciplines that question the conditions of animal agency. Although the field of animal studies does at times communicate with more radical political and activist-oriented fields, the first tends to favor the study of agency, often (though not always) at the expense of the analysis of global history in which this power is inscribed. Such an analysis neglects the situation of oppression that often prevents the expression of this agency. The second approach—radical and explicitly political activism, including but not limited to critical animal studies—contrary to more mainstream animal studies, is dominated by activists who contribute to showing the suffering of animals. They often display it in an inoffensive way, with the aim of educational awareness, through legal and if necessary (when laws are unjust), sometimes illegal means. The legality or illegality is therefore not enough to inform about the effectiveness of activism.

This chapter is divided into two main parts. The first deals with the use of the concept of agency in the social sciences, and more particularly in animal studies. Some epistemological approaches are appraised based on the work of the Belgian historian Violette Pouillard (2019), the American politician James C. Scott (1987) and the French philosopher Elsa Dorlin (2017). As for the second part, we deal with the use of the concept of agency within the political struggle. To do so, we base our discussion on the distinction between two discursive and political registers that coexist historically, as well as on their respective strategic effects.

Due to formal constraints and being fluent French speakers, we have translated the French quotations into English in this chapter. We hope that our translations are as faithful as possible to the original meaning.

SOCIAL SCIENCES AND AGENCY

In animal studies as a field, animals have become historical actors since the Latourian paradigm of actants has been inserted into them. Latour considers as actants those whose action can modify or make others act—i.e., human, non-human, ideas, objects, microbes, etc. Through their actions and what they make others do, *actants* become actors, assembling collectives that form the social (Latour, 2007, p. 103). Nevertheless, this paradigm as applied in *animal studies* has had the effect of placing animals as actors in the same way as other *actants*/actors, to the detriment of their specificities of experiencing pain and pleasure (Pouillard, 2019).

As Violette Pouillard (2019) points out in her book *Histoire des zoos par les animaux: im périalisme, contrôle, conservation,* the turning point of agency as conceived in the Latourian paradigm is a strange generosity that can give as well as take. Pouillard rightly points out that the symmetry that Latour poses between humans and nonhumans is analytical, not political or moral, even though the approach can change the political. Thus, Latour is an invitation to consider animal agency, not an end, and the form of the latter depends on what one does with the invitation (*ibid.*). Following in the footsteps of Pouillard, we write this article in order partially to respond to the invitation.

First, we would like to briefly present the point of view we share with Pouillard regarding the Latourian paradigm deployed in animal studies by authors such as Jocelyne Porcher, Donna Haraway and Vinciane Despret. These authors like to work on seductive assemblages where there is cooperation, such as attempts to build a better world. They like to work on dynamic scenes where all the actors deploy their agency. But in her study of zoos, Pouillard (2019) reveals what lies behind these scenes: silences, boredom, confinement and coercion often necessary to the materialization of these dynamic scenes. While there may be some points of agreement, these authors and their work do not go far enough in promoting animal agency.

For example, a study of a zoo cannot only show the positive aspects of a relationship between a caretaker and a chimpanzee—the walks, the ways in which both learn from each other, and so forth. Similarly, taking into account the moments of resistance deployed by the animals would not be enough, even if it would bring a counterbalance to the "beautiful relations." Note that whatever scene is analyzed, we are faced with the realities of the daily life of animals in zoos punctuated by boredom, confinement and solitary nights and winters. In other words, animal daily life is made up of non-dynamic scenes, which are therefore uninteresting for the Latourian paradigm. This paradigm does not allow us to capture the real, lived animal experience in a zoo, and this extends to many other animal experiences of life in farms, circuses, animal entertainment parks, etc.

Moreover, this paradigm refuses to show the suffering and therefore the victimization of animals in the above-mentioned institutions. In trying to raise animal agency at all costs, victimization escapes the eye. Based on this observation, Pouillard (2019, p. 13) points out four biases relating to the avoidance of the issue of suffering:

- *Bias of complacency*: not looking at suffering allows us to focus on anthropozoological dynamics rather than on rupturing the human-animal binary.
- *Academic bias*: Suffering is an object from which many academics turn away, who consider it not "cold" enough (e.g., too political), as if it were not about corporality in the broadest sense, but about feelings; not justice, but sentimentality, and not good enough to think about, too far removed from the beautiful assemblages of Latour and Haraway.
- *Social bias*: The emphasis is on resistance fighters who are free from suffering, who are powerful and strong, who escape, who have broken their destiny, because we prefer them to crushed existences.
- *Speciesist bias*: Would we have any idea, before examining the lives and deaths of human slaves—the uprooting, the punishments, the diseases, the mortality rates, all the mechanics of dislocation, of giving a virtual monopoly in writing to the development of the best master-slave relations, to the resistance and strategies of the slaves—of the acts of a few who have been able to exploit the system to their advantage and of those, even rarer, who have been able to overthrow it?

(Pouillard, 2019, p. 13, our translation)

By criticizing animal studies as a field of exploring human-animal relations in this way, Pouillard works on some common ground with critical animal studies. Indeed, both identify some issues with how researchers within animal studies as a field are apolitical and often support the keeping of animals in zoos, laboratories, *et cetera*, and how animal studies conceptually approaches the study of nonhuman animals in a detached and distant way.

Furthermore, Erika Cudworth (2015) points out that stressing the observation on domesticated nonhumans cannot lead to a better understanding of "what might constitute 'liberation' for other species we might never know" (p. 299).

Indeed, our approach of "liberation" contains a human-centered bias as we often work only with nonhuman animals that get along with us human animals.

BUILDING WITH POUILLARD, SCOTT AND DORLIN

As we are aware that Pouillard's and Elsa Dorlin's books are not translated in English, we'd like to introduce them. Pouillard's research concerns the history of human-animal relationships and of wildlife control and protection policies from the early 19th century onward. Her last book (Pouillard, 2019) is a history of zoos and particularly how animal studies are involved in that escalation of violence (for a CAS approach to violence against animals, see Wadiwel, 2015). Pouillard also points out how some concepts used in a Latourian paradigm to study human-animal relationships can be speciesist. One of these concepts discussed is that of agency, the subject of this chapter. Furthermore, Pouillard's approach is considerably influenced by the historical approach of history from below, also known as people's history. This type of history mainly consists of not thinking from the point of view of the masters, capitalists or dominators but by the one of slaves, workers and dominated (Zinn, 2005). Violette Pouillard continues this by adding that studying institutions that involve human-animal relationships would mean being by the side of the animals. This explains her book's title that could be translated to mean: *A History of Zoos by Animals* or *An Animal's History of Zoos*. As for Elsa Dorlin, she is a Foucauldian philosopher who reflects on race and gender in an intersectional approach. What is interesting for us in her work is her thoughts about the modern subject as we will see later. A translation of the prologue, "Ce que peut un corps," to Elsa Dorlin's book *Se Défendre: Une Philosophie de la Violence* (translation: *Defending Yourself: A Philosophy of Violence*) is available online (Dorlin, 2019).

Let there be no misunderstanding: our proposal is not to think of animals only as victims. Rather, our proposal is to broaden the notion of agency to a set of behaviors characterized by suffering and a lack of dynamism. Agency is not only the development of privileged relationships with a guardian or visible and extraordinary resistance. Agency is also made up of solitary nights in the empty cell, of resilience, discouragement, prostrations, and turned backs. As Pouillard (2019) testifies, even sitting around doing "nothing" is already doing something.

With this expansion of the concepts of agency and resistance, as much as the infinite power of animals can be shown, the control devices that render them powerless—often cutting them off from their inner space—can also be unveiled. The power of animals is no longer only expressed by exceptional events such as the escape of Tyke (1974–1994) in Honolulu in 1994. The gorilla Horatio of the Ménagerie des Plantes de Paris also enters the ranks of the resistance fighters, even though his mode of resistance was prostration, stereotypical behavior and gnawing his fingers until he tore his own flesh (Pouillard, 2019, pp. 320–321). This inclusive gesture makes it possible not to reproduce the social bias noted by Pouillard mentioned earlier.

The American anarchist, political scientist and anthropologist James C. Scott had already understood that the modes of resistance of subordinates were not the same as those presented by intellectuals and elites as being political. Scott considers each of the following behaviors as forms of resistance, termed "weapons of the weak" (1987): "Faking ignorance, rejection of commands, the slowdown, foot-dragging, no work without adequate food, refusal to work in the heat of the day, taking breaks without permission, rejection of overtime, vocal complaints, open pilfering, secret pilfering, rebuffing new tasks, false compliance, breaking equipment, escape, and direct confrontation" (cited in Hribal, 2007, p. 103). Scott shows us that we have given attention to the status of resistance only at the tip of the iceberg: that of direct and visible resistance, and that of large mobilizations. This position discriminates against the resistance deployed by the majority of the world: the subordinates, a category to which animals belong. They are those who cannot visibly defend themselves without extreme consequences. Think of the 86 bullets that Tyke took when he fled, or Horatio who was separated from his comrade because they developed an aggressive resistance together. It was a result of this separation that Horatio fell into the abyss of withdrawal. Most of the time the agency deployed by the animals whose lives are bruised by confinement remains within the order of the infra-political and inward-looking.

Finally, the advantage of this approach is not so much to be able to show the suffering but rather to be able to detect the control and oppression mechanisms thought up and put in place by the institutions that place animals in captivity such as zoos, circuses, animal parks, farms, etc. (see Colling, 2021). For example, Horatio and his companion showed visible resistance: they wounded a guard and charged against the gates when some people approached. In response, the institution separated the two gorillas, accentuating their confinement, and Horatio fell into the abyss of withdrawal (Hribal, 2007). These institutions are veritable machines for thinking about captivity and, therefore, the construction of powerlessness.

In an attempt to define the "modern subject" in her book *Se défendre* (our translation: *Defend Itself*), the French philosopher Elsa Dorlin notes that the modern subject has been defined "by its capacity to defend itself" (2017). She adds that, "This capacity for self-defense has also become a criterion used to discriminate between those who are truly subjects and the others" (*Ibid.*, p. 8). Despite the fact that animals are completely excluded from her analysis, it is revealing that she manages to talk about animals without seeking to do so. Indeed, we are not inventing anything new if we assert that animals are not considered as subjects in the institutions we are talking about. These institutions continually put into place devices that diminish, annihilate, deviate and delegitimize the capacity for self-defense of animals. They continually hold a Damocles sword over the heads of captive animals and instill in them their inability to defend themselves, creating a radical impotence. By speaking of oppressed humans in such a powerful way, Dorlin could not avoid showing the oppression to which nonhuman animals are subjected.

The social and historical sciences must make it a point of honor to unveil these devices, which are not at all metaphysical, but very concrete actions, field actions: separating comrades, building ever higher walls, electrifying fences, holding the bullock firmly and continuously, allowing oneself to murder if the animalized body invites itself into a humanized space where nothing is provided for them.

AGENCY AND ANIMAL RIGHTS ACTIVISM

In the animal activism field in French-speaking regions, the liberal and moralist approach is hegemonic. The majority of animal activist groups are imbued with the vision of speciesism inherited from Peter Singer (1975). According to Singer (1975), "speciesists allow the interests of their own species to override the greater interests of members of other species" (pp. 8–9). With the acceptance of this definition, the problem identified is individualized. Individual prejudices and moral mistrust of animals are seen as the main limits to be overcome. This gives rise to many welfarist animal groups that raise awareness, educate, and inform individuals about animal suffering, which is accompanied by the idea that if people are aware, they will change their attitudes. Also, in their use of legal, conventional modes of action, they demand animal "welfare" and a "more humane" treatment of animals. If some actors resort to civil disobedience where the means are not entirely legal, often the action is limited to the same objective of informing and raising awareness. As David Nibert (2002) argues, this understanding of speciesism betrays a confusion between prejudice and structure. The foundations of violence against animals and its reproduction in the dominant culture are indeed not to be found merely in individual attitudes. They are not the primary causes but only the ideological effect of our institutional systems and economic structures. Individual attitudes are secondary; on their own they do not significantly challenge the underlying structures and social institutions. That is why, according for animal liberation activists, it is of little importance to raise awareness among individuals if no action is taken at the level of those who orchestrate and reproduce domination. By focusing on structures and institutions rather than on individuals, a different strategy of struggle is needed, and the anarchist collective 269 Libération Animale (or, 269 LA)—not to be confused with 269 Life—is precisely in line with this strategy. Their action is not embedded in the individualizing guilt of individuals—which constrains action in the harmless distribution of leaflets, demonstrations, happenings, petitions, etc.—but in the concrete liberation of oppressed animals by targeting the institutions responsible for this domination. As Anthony Nocella II and Steve Best (2004) explain about the Animal Liberation Front (ALF), "the movement for animal and earth liberation are a continuation of the American culture of rights, democracy, civil disobedience, and direct action, as they expand the struggle to a far broader constituency" (p. 16). This is precisely where 269 LA finds itself: in the tradition of anarchist revolutionaries such as the ALF in fights for justice through direct action strategies. This is why it is relevant to bring 269 LA's ideas in this discussion about the concept of agency. Indeed, their ideas are in line with the ones supported by critical animal studies such as the theory-to-practice approach, intersectionality, solidarity and total liberation among others (Nocella II et al., 2013; Nocella II et al., 2019).

The subjugation of animals is perceived as a social war that requires an offensive strategic positioning. As Foucault explains in *Il faut défendre la société: Cours au Collège de France* (translation: *Why Society Must Be Defended: Course at the College de France*) (2012) the State introduces into the field of life a biological fracture between what must live and what must die. It is against this logic of inclusion and exclusion that the struggle must be waged, and it is this conception of anti-speciesism that distinguishes the collective from other animalist groups in the French-speaking world.

In historical social struggles, there are two registers that characterize action: the register of the politicization of suffering and that of the politicization of power (autonomy) (See texts of 269 LA on their Facebook page). This analytical distinction implies different strategic options.

REGISTER OF SUFFERING

The politicization of suffering is generally associated with a politicization of the negative. In the animal cause, it positions humans to speak instead of animals as if animals cannot already "speak" for themselves. Insisting on the suffering of animals by displaying it publicly is a form of action in the negative because activists are content to show suffering, to stage it, but remain far from the animals themselves. These activists do not exert any force to resist with the oppressed. The latter are made invisible, forgotten, hidden behind the bodies of the activists, their posters, and their slogans. They put on a show while the animals are exploited, captivated, abused, and crushed in the shadows of institutions.

These modes of action claim to politicize the issue by emotionally challenging public opinion and are based on the triple presupposition that Dorlin presents in *Se Défendre* (2017): (i) it is by making a problem visible that it becomes real; (ii) it is by mobilizing emotions and in particular empathy that the reality of a phenomenon becomes a reality for everyone; and finally, (iii) it is by showing the consequences of an act or practice that the perpetrators of these acts are touched as moral subjects, likely to become aware of the invisibility, illegality, immorality or danger of their actions.

It is one thing for the problem to become real for all and to make moral subjects aware of it; it is quite another for the reality of the problem to be reversed, transformed and fought against. If the politicization of animal suffering makes a problem visible, it does so in a public space in which the presence of the oppressed—the animals—is prohibited. The animal is presented as spectacle, they are given to be seen, as in the campaigns on violence against women studied by Dorlin, as "captured in a mummified present forever" (2017, p. 159). The most vivid and spontaneous scenes are eternally frozen in animal bodies, prostrate, bloody, beaten, dead bodies, escaping all reflection, all resistance, all power. No element reminds us of the complexity of reality, of the flesh of life. As if animals were all condemned to this fatal fate out of weakness, vulnerability, and passivity. The exhibition of suffering systematically refers to the powerlessness of oppressed individuals; it reifies their existence in passive and weak states.

REGISTER OF POWER

Non-human individuals are not simply passive victims who suffer oppression. They are certainly constrained in powerful speciesist structures that reassign them to their animality and often prevent the expression of their agency (Colling, 2021), but they are also something more. Introducing animals into politics by penetrating institutions to resist with them, hearing their cries and observing the muscular force with which they resist, is to testify to their power to act; additionally, it is to observe animals as something other than bruised. The anarchist anti-speciesism of 269 LA participates in the politicization of animal power. By being accomplices of the oppressed, of their liberation and resistance, and by developing territories on which the animals can live free, they make concrete a reality that contradicts the fatal destiny promised to animals (for more in-depth discussion of 269 LA, see Jacquemin, 2019).

The space of resistance that is created allows concrete existences to flourish. For a single life saved is already a life worth living. On the sanctuary, the animals bear the physio-logical and genetic marks of the oppressor; their weight far exceeds their height, their life expectancy is uncertain, some con-tract diseases linked to breeding, others die an early death, etc., but they draw from what the system has not taken from them—to walk, run, play, and flour-ish. Every day they show their specificity, their desires, and their habits. They find the possibility to socialize and live by making friendships or quarrels. The politicization of animal power does not therefore meet a strategic requirement in the fight because it makes it possible, by the means it uses, to achieve the concrete emancipation of non-human individuals. Indeed, this register allows the substitution of the powerful and resistant animal for that of a wounded victim. But it is not simply out of a concern to "show" the animals in a different way that this register takes place. It is necessary in order to bring about, by being an accomplice to this power, the conditions required for animals to fully enjoy their power.

CONCLUSION

As we have shown, *animal studies* attempts to hide animal suffering for the benefit of agency. Mainstream discourse and welfarist practices give some importance to suffering but when they take up the issue of resistance, they only take into account visible, extraordinary resistance.

The effect of the Animal Studies movement is to render invisible the power relations and practices of control that dictate the lives of animals, that render them powerless and push them into their final strongholds. This is why we have proposed to take suffering into account: it makes visible again what has been made invisible.

As for practices, including discourse, that focus only on suffering, the effect dwindles down to ineffective action strategies that dictate our vision of animals as individuals who do not resist, who only suffer. The practices of 269 Libération Animale allow us to break out of this vision in order to show how powerful ani-mals can be when they are out of captivity and obtain absolute control over their bodies. Thus, it is a question of co-resisting with animals within the institutions where such structural oppression takes place (slaughterhouses, farms, etc.), rather than only through indirect means—such as street protests that fight for animal rights from afar. As previously mentioned, agency and suffering are two sides of the same coin: that of domination. With this in mind, whether in consideration of the struggle or of the research, the two sides remain dialectical. This is why the theory-to-practice approach used in critical animal studies is fundamental. It involves back-and-forth iterations between theory and practice, between scholar-ship and activism (Best et al., 2007).

REFERENCES

Best, S., & Nocella II, A. (2004). *Terrorists or freedom fighters? Reflections on the liberation of animals.* Lantern Books.

Best, S ., Nocella II, A., Kahn, R., Gigliotti, C., & Kemmerer, L. (2007). Introducing critical animal studies. *Journal for Critical Animal Studies, 5*(1), 4–5.

Colling, Sarat. (2021). *Animal resistance in the global capitalist era.* Michigan State University Press.

Cudworth, E. (2015). Intersectionality, species and social domination. In A. J. Nocella II, R. J. White, & E. Cudworth (Eds.), *Anarchism and animal liberation: Essays on complementary elements of total liberation* (pp. 97–103). McFarland & Co Inc.

Dorlin, E. (2017), *Se défendre.* La découverte. Collection Zones.

Dorlin, E. (2019, autumn). What a body can do. *Radical Philosophy, 2*(5). Accessed December 13, 2020. (https://www.radicalphilosophy.com/article/what-a-body-can-do)

Foucault, M. (2012). *Il faut défendre la société: Cours au Collège de France. Cours du 17 mars 1976.* Seuil. Collection Hautes Etudes.

Hribal, J. (2007). Animals, agency, and class: Writing the history of animals from below. *Human Ecology Review, 14*(1), 101–112.

Jacquemin, K. (2019). *Clandestins: ethnographie d'un sanctuaire.* Université de Mons. Accessed March 24, 2020. (https://www.academia.edu/41464454/Clandestins_ethnographie_dun_sanctuaire)

Latour, B. (2007). *Changer de société, refaire de la sociologie.* La découverte. Collection poche/Sciences humaines et sociales.

Nibert, D. (2002). *Animal rights/human Rights: Entanglements of oppression and liberation.* Rowman & Littlefield.

Nocella II, A. J., & George, A. (Eds.). (2019). *Intersectionality of critical animal studies: A historical collection.* Peter Lang.

Nocella II, A. J., Sorenson, J., Socha, K., & Matsuoka, A. (Eds.). (2013). *Defining critical animal studies: An intersectional social justice approach for liberation.* Peter Lang.

Pouillard, V. (2019). *Histoire des zoos par les animaux: contrôle, impérialisme, conservation.* Champ Vallon. Collection L'environnement a une histoire.

Scott, J. C. (1987). *Weapons of the weak: Everyday forms of peasant resistance.* Yale University Press.

Singer, P. (1975). *La libération animale.* Payot. Collection Petite Bibliothèque Payot.

Wadiwel, D. (2015). *The war against animals.* Brill/Rodopi.

Zinn, H. (2005). *A people's history of the United States.* Harper Perennial Modern Classics.

CHAPTER THREE

"It's a Privilege": A Critical Examination of University Students' Perspectives of Animal Experimentation in Science Education

ALAINA INTERISANO

Across North America the number of animals used for research, education and testing continues to increase annually, despite the fact that the technology and availability of non-animal alternatives in science has improved and advanced over the past several decades. This increase runs contrary to the principles that are often propagated by the scientific community of replacing, reducing and refining the use of animals in science. The socialization process of animal experimentation begins through pedagogy, making the university an ideal site for examining the reproduction of animal models as the status quo method in education, research and testing. Here, I examine student perspectives and experiences of engaging in animal experimentation, as a part of their education, through six in-depth interviews with Biology and Neuroscience undergraduate students at Brock University, located in Southern Ontario, Canada. In understanding students' experiences, and how pedagogy affects their perceptions of this practice, my findings illuminate how the perceived necessity of animal models is maintained and reproduced through a speciesist pedagogy. Student perspectives are important in the conversations around animal experimentation in education, as they are the beneficiaries of this pedagogy, and therefore, their voices should be centralized in the discussion. Pedersen (2010) argues that discussions of animals and human-animal relations throughout education construct how we perceive animals, which subsequently affects how we treat them. While exploring the practice of dissection, compared to non-animal alternative technologies, Waters et al. (2011) found that students preferred the method that they were predominantly taught with. Therefore, the experimentation practices learned in university form an important site in the knowledge development of future researchers, as this knowledge can significantly influence their techniques, values, beliefs and treatment of nonhuman animals moving forward. Using past studies of students' perspectives on animal experimentation and the emerging literature on the interconnection of pedagogy and animal experimentation, I extend and complicate the findings of several foundational pieces (e.g. Birke et al., 2007; Capaldo, 2004; Eadie, 2011; Deguchi et al., 2012; Pedersen, 2002, 2004, 2010). In addressing student experiences and perceptions of animal experimentation, I begin by analyzing how students rationalize and make sense of their use of animals, followed by a critical examination of how students' perceptions are shaped. Before proceeding, it is important to note that the term "animal experimentation" describes the biological, psychological, and medical scientific uses of live animals in research and educational settings (Monamy, 2009). I use the term animal experimentation rather than dissection or vivisection because not all educational uses of animals result in the complete dissection and/or cutting of live animals (i.e., behavioral and psychological experiments).

RATIONALIZATIONS AND THE ABSOLUTION OF CULPABILITY

As previous research has supported, rationalizing the use of animals in education may require a number of processes of socialization and desensitization to occur, such as objectification, emotional detachment or ambivalence, and strategies for absolving guilt and responsibility in the animals' harm and death (e.g. Birke, 2012; Pedersen, 2010; Arluke & Hafferty, 1996). As outlined by Arluke and Hafferty (1996), the process of absolution, for students engaged in animal experimentation, is done through a denial of wrongfulness and responsibility in the experiments and deaths of animals. One particularly noteworthy absolution strategy identified was how students establish absolution based on the principle that if animals are anesthetized, and do not appear to feel pain, then whatever transpires during the experiment is acceptable (Arluke & Hafferty, 1996). Students' perceptions of the animals' inability to feel pain, were key in my interviews for accepting their involvement in the experiments and rationalizing the continuation of animal models in education and research. One participant, Olivia, highlighted that once an animal is anesthetized "they won't experience any pain," which therefore "mitigates any harm to [the animals]." While this is completely devoid of consideration of the emotional and psychological harm that nonhuman animals experience in labs, it works as an absolution strategy for students to be able to participate in the experiments without a sense of guilt or wrongdoing. Interestingly, even when the animals are not anesthetized, students still used this absolution technique; Layla noted that before an animal is injected with a substance in her labs the animals are spun around to "stun" them which she felt mitigated pain, while another student, Mary, claimed that the during her work as a research assistant she was told that decapitation, without anesthesia, was humane and resulted in the least amount of suffering for the animals. In both of these cases, the uneasiness of harming animals was mitigated once the students *believed* the animal was not in pain, even in circumstances where the animals were not anesthetized and the inability to feel pain was not guaranteed, as it offset any reservations they may have felt about what was being done to the animals.

Arluke and Hafferty (1996) expand on their discussion of absolutions to include that—in addition to them being used to remove stigma and permit a moral acceptability of questionable practices—absolutions also "morally elevate the behavior, making it an honor or privilege to perform while leaving one's moral self completely unscathed if not somewhat enhanced" (p. 222). This element of absolutions is clearly identifiable among the students interviewed, as half of the students noted that it was a great 'privilege' to perform animal experimentation in their education. Olivia distinguished it as a privilege, not a right, to work with the animals, explaining "we're taught that not every school has that opportunity, and to be cognizant that we are very privileged to have [the animals]." Several other students also related their experience of engaging in animal experimentation as a privilege, noting that students at other larger schools do not get the same opportunity to use animal models due to larger class sizes. Another participant, Layla, understood the privilege of using animals to be a result of the instructors having such a high level of trust in their students, and expressed honor at being considered qualified enough to use them. Interestingly, in addition to students feeling privileged in their ability to use nonhuman animals in their education, many students also attributed privilege to certain aspects of the animals' lives. Students routinely drew attention to the perception that animals have a better life in the labs than they would outside of captivity, noting that they're fed, cared for daily and housed safely. One student, Cara, even noted that she believed that the life expectancy of animals was far greater in animal research than in their natural environments. These assertions suggest that the freedom of animals from captivity, harm and death, do not measure up to the quality of life that students believe the animals experience in the labs. The absurdities of these claims reveal them to be a means of absolution, as most of the students portrayed the captivity of lab animals as beneficial and for their own good, in spite of the harm and ultimate death they face. In actuality, this perception is likely another attempt to create grounds for acceptance of this practice, by positioning the animals as privileged to be the recipients of care, food and housing over noncaptive members of their species, while denying culpability in any pain and death that they will inevitably experience.

In another instance, Olivia explained that she believed animals are not sacrificed or killed at the end of an experiment, rather they enter into a peaceful retirement, where "after whatever they need to be used for has happened ... they will basically just live out the rest of their days." By using the term 'retirement' to describe an animal's ending in the lab, this student was obscuring the deaths of the lab animals and imposing a silver lining at the end of the experimentation process, one that was denied by other students. Similarly, Mary and Cara both depicted examples of animal privilege through purported superior treatment of animals. As Mary explained, "they [instructors] always tell us that the air that [animals] breathe is cleaner than ours." This notion depicts animals as having superior air quality to humans, which according to Mary was representative of their high quality of life and care in the lab. Furthermore, Cara illustrated an instructor's account of past research on cats, in which researchers would feed the cats their own lunch if and when the cat food did not arrive on time. This example suggests a form of sacrifice on the part of the researchers, and an attempt by the student to elevate the moral positionality of the experimenter. In reference to the context of both Mary and Cara's comments, both used these accounts as anecdotal evidence that animals are privileged to be receiving such outstanding care, and to offset the negative perceptions associated with the inherently harmful and lethal animal experiments they engaged in.

Additionally, in an interview with Layla, she mentioned that while she was hesitant to engage in animal experimentation, she found solace after speaking with an instructor regarding the animals' care and transportation to the labs. Layla states that

> If they [the animals] were treated really badly, I would be completely against it. But since ... [the instructor has] shown me that they get the top of the line treatment - they're flown in, they get their own plane, they drive in limos - I feel like that kind of reassured me.

In this example, Layla equated the privilege of private and luxurious transportation with "top of the line treatment" for the animals in the lab. Even if this was indeed true, it is difficult to assert that animals transported in crates and cages, and who have no conception of anthropocentric methods of transport, would benefit in any way from a private plane or limousine. Nonetheless, this instructor used this discourse to create a more palatable picture for Layla to digest, by exaggerating and falsifying certain aspects of the lab animals' lives and bestowing a misleading position of privilege onto the animals. Consequently, when these strategies are employed, it is likely to neutralize and absolve students' guilt or reservations about using animals in classroom experiments, appeasing them with the perception of animals' exceptional care and treatment.

PEDAGOGICAL FALLACIES AND MISCONCEPTIONS

Along with the exaggerated claims of privileged care and treatment, students also expressed other misleading claims in their rationalization of animal use. Firstly, when asked what they were taught about the transferability of animal data to human conditions, students insisted that animal models are by and large successful in providing data that applies directly to humans, and that animals are vital for medical breakthroughs. Several students indicated that since various animal species share similarities to us physiologically, it allows for transferable results to be extrapolated to human conditions. As Marcus explained,

> I don't know the percentages or statistics behind it, but I do know that the reason rats are experimented on is because their brain structure is similar to that of humans, so that way whatever treatment would affect the rats, would affect humans in a similar manner.

This perspective is similar to the accounts of other students, who used this to rationalize and justify their use of animals. Another student, Cara, even went as far as to assert that "we would never do research on something if it couldn't be generalizable to humans." Additionally, the majority of students adamantly asserted that without animal experimentation and the transferability of animal models to human conditions, lifesaving medical breakthroughs would not exist. However, these claims are highly contentious, as many notable scholars and scientists (e.g., Anderegg et al., 2002; Birke, 2012; Fadali, 1996; Folescu et al., 2013; Greek & Greek, 2002) have argued the exact opposite, denouncing animal experimentation for its unreliability and poor transferability, and asserting that the high failure rates have actually misled many scientific discoveries, which students did not seem to be aware of. For a more comprehensive discussion on animal studies that have misled science and medicine, see Anderegg et al. (2002), Fadali (1996) and Monamy (2009). Furthermore, according to the Canadian Council on Animal Care (2020), nearly half of animal experimentation in Canada (48%) relates to 'fundamental research', which according to Greek and Greek (2010) is synonymous with basic or curiosity-driven research, whereby experimental work is conducted for the acquirement of new knowledge without any specific use or application in mind. Therefore, nearly half of animal experiments conducted are not necessarily contributing to medical breakthroughs, and when they seemingly do, it is often not clear if such achievements were dependent on animal models, or if these models were merely included at some point of the research process (Matthews, 2008). Additionally, due to publication bias we are led to believe that animal experimentation is more significant than it really is, as the many failings of animal experimentation are not published and are thus underestimated. While animal models have played a part in the advancement of scientific knowledge, there is also no way of knowing where we would be without animal data in science and medicine (Greek & Greek, 2010). Students are subsequently misled through pedagogy to equate animal experimentation with lifesaving cures for human illnesses (Greek & Greek, 2010), as these claims dismiss the mounting evidence to the contrary. Birke (2012) posits that when students are taught that animal experimentation has been and continues to be our only salvation from suffering, they justify these harmful practices in order to achieve this. As students are taught that animal experimentation is an essential part of science and medicine, it becomes easier to rationalize and support the use of animals in education, research and testing.

Another sweeping claim insisted by most of the students was that the voices of opposition to animal experimentation exclusively come from animal liberation communities, presupposing a unanimous agreement from the scientific community on this practice. While there are certainly proponents of animal experimentation in the scientific community, and opponents of this practice within the animal liberation communities, this assumption disregards the existence and perspectives of the many outspoken opponents within the scientific community (e.g. Anderegg et al., 2002; Birke et al., 2007; Fadali, 1996; Greek & Greek, 2010; Lankford, 2009). Students echoed the sentiment made by Cara that, "it'd be hard to find someone who is very against it" in the scientific community, asserting instead that in the debates on animal experimentation, People for the Ethical Treat of Animals (PETA), vegans and animal liberationists are the opposition fighting against animal use. When asked if the debates surrounding animal experimentation are ever mentioned in class, and in what context, Cara explained, "yes absolutely. Every professor will mention it, because it's offensive of course to the professors. People basically calling them villains because they're using animals." This suggests that the pedagogy that students are experiencing is problematically one sided, with no mention of the legitimate critiques and bioethical concerns from those within the scientific community. Therefore, students are misled when the arguments of scientific opposition are omitted, as it leads students to homogenize the perspectives of those within the scientific community towards animal experimentation, in favor of this practice. Additionally, this assumption is problematic because it positions only those who are not directly involved in animal experimentation as the opposition, making it easier to discredit their views and position their voices as ignorant outsiders in this discussion. Due to these perceptions, students contended that "science people," as Mary puts it, understand that animal experimentation is acceptable and necessary, whereas those outside of the sciences who oppose animal experimentation are simply misinformed. Cara in particular felt strongly that the opposition to animal experimentation is coming from those who are uneducated on the practice, explaining that "most people who are very against it are also not very well educated in what happens." Therefore, despite the fact that students appear unaware of the internal debate on animal experimentation, particularly the opposition from scientists and researchers within the scientific community, some students assert that it is the opposition who are not well educated on this practice. Additionally, Cara added that in response to confronting these debates, instructors have explicitly told students not to engage with those who oppose it, which creates a further divide between the proponents and opponents of animal experimentation by deterring dialogue and debate. Furthermore, this insinuates that those who oppose animal experimentation are simply too far removed from, and unable to comprehend, the scientific rationale, which once again ignores the countless scientists and researchers with extensive scientific knowledge who oppose animal experimentation and dissuades students from exploring alternative perspectives. Subsequently, this mentality of ignoring opposition to a controversial practice diminishes transparency, which makes it increasingly difficult to challenge and promote change through constructive dialogue.

Finally, in all of the interviews, students described what I interpret to be false dichotomies regarding human-animal relations in the sciences. In connection to the usefulness of animal models in predicting human responses, each student interviewed equated animal experimentation as necessary to avoid human experimentation, positioning animal models as the only viable alternative to human models. This dichotomy between animal models and human models was insinuated with statements such as, "it's really important to use animals, as opposed to testing on people" (Cara), or "all of those experiments have been occurring on animals because they don't want to do it on humans" (Marcus). Therefore, participants' perceptions of animals in science are formed around the belief that since it is morally reprehensible to perform human experimentation, animal experimentation is the closest acceptable option, rationalizing the continuation of animal models. These presumptions, that animal experimentation is used to spare humans from experimentation, are problematic for two main reasons. Firstly, they dismiss the many alternative methods that are successfully used in replacement of human and animal experimentation, such as computer simulations and models, statistical modeling, non-invasive imaging techniques, epidemiology and cell cultures (Folescu et al., 2013). Secondly, these perceptions also assume that human experimentation does not occur in conjunction with animal experimentation, when in actuality, human experimentation has always, and continues to, accompany animal experimentation in some way (Luke, 2007). Through historical examples such as the Tuskegee syphilis studies, and current examples of clinical drug trials in the Global South, we see how socially disempowered human groups have been and are still being used for experimental purposes. Current experimental drug trials often target countries experiencing economic and political instability, and are often criticized for lacking adequate informed consent and exploiting marginalized and vulnerable racialized populations (e.g., Nundy & Gulhati, 2005;

Kamat, 2014). While human experimentation does not currently occur in the same context or with the same open acceptability as animal experimentation, it is important to highlight its presence. Therefore, the presumption that animal experimentation needs to continue as a substitute for human experimentation is misinformed, as it ignores the cases of human experimentation that have historically and presently been used alongside animal experimentation, as well as the available non-animal alternatives. Furthermore, as a result of this mentality, that animal experimentation must be used as opposed to human experimentation, students expressed a false dichotomy between human health and animal lives. This is significant in understanding how students' perceptions of animals as research objects are shaped, specifically in how they rationalize animal experimentation through these beliefs. Olivia noted that we must understand the "trade-offs," while Mary rhetorically asked, "whose life is valued more, humans or animals?" In both cases, students depict a choice between human health and animal lives, while also directly linking the pursuit of human health and wellbeing with the practice of animal experimentation. Therefore, these comments falsely convey human health and animal lives as mutually exclusive, when in actuality many alternatives to animal models can be used to benefit human health, in addition to protecting animals from harmful experimental procedures.

MARGINALIZATION OF ALTERNATIVES

Once the conversations turned to available alternatives to animal models, it became apparent that the general consensus among these students was that successful alternatives do not currently exist to replace animal models, and that more time and advanced technology was needed. While some studies have suggested that students using alternatives to animal experimentation tend to prefer and perform equal to, if not better than, students using animal models (e.g., Pedersen, 2002; Wang, 2001), students asserted that whatever alternatives are available are inferior to animal use. When asked if alternatives were offered for students who did not want to participate in animal experiments, the student responses were quite mixed. Some students claimed that there are alternatives available in certain cases, while others had never heard of any mentioned. Mary stated, that in one of her labs an alternative was offered for an experiment on a sheep brain; yet, no alternative was offered for a subsequent experiment on crayfish in the same course. Additionally, Cara noted, "in some classes it's not made available ... we're told this is a lab-based course and there's no alternative ... if you don't feel comfortable, don't take this class; you should drop this class." In both of these accounts, it is evident that the availability of alternatives to animal experimentation is dependent on the experiment and can vary greatly from course to course.

Additionally, students mentioned that even if an alternative was available, they are not well advertised by instructors; as Marcus explained, "they're there, but they haven't really given us a 'if you don't want to do the [experiment], you can do this'. They [the instructors] haven't come up front with that." Additionally, Cara noted that she thinks some instructors might accommodate requests for alternatives, "but it wasn't advertised." This explains the uncertainty that some students expressed when asked about available alternatives in their labs, as it appears that even when there may be an alternative option, instructors do not seem to be explicitly presenting these options to students, effectively marginalizing the alternatives that are available. Furthermore, as Mary explained, even when their lab was formally presented with information of an alternative online module, the instructor "put a negative spin on doing that", with the caveat that students who chose the alternative would not get as much out of the assignment. This suggests that alternatives to animal experimentation are overtly delegitimized by some instructors in the offering of alternatives as a replacement to animal models, as well as covertly marginalized when they are not explicitly or clearly advertised to students. After having the instructor openly discourage the educational efficacy of the alternative option, Mary recalled that when one student tried the alternative

> she didn't feel like she got anything out of it … she thought she could just get away with doing a computer module and get as much out of it … but then again, she wasn't doing anything so that makes sense.

In this example Mary equated an alternative computer model to doing nothing, suggesting a perceived lack of legitimacy in the offered alternative, which was likely influenced by how the alternative was presented to the students in the first place. This demonstrates that when instructors delegitimize alternatives to animal experimentation, students are subsequently taught that non-animal alternatives are inferior to animal models, which influences their overall perception of animal experimentation as the best available option. Moreover, by not advertising alternatives, or by presenting them in a negative way, instructors are likely discouraging students from coming forward with their reservations of animal experimentation and their potential interest in alternative methods.

COERCIVE AND SPECIESIST PEDAGOGIES

While none of the students interviewed had ever opted out of an experiment presented to them in their classes, Layla reflected on an experience she had with an instructor regarding her discomfort with animal experimentation. Layla explained that when she approached her instructor about her concerns, and the possibility of an alternative assignment, the conversation quickly turned into an attempt to persuade and coerce her into doing the experiment despite her discomfort. Layla explained that at the end of their discussion the instructor conceded that an alternative could be arranged "as a last resort" but did not recommend it because the alternative would not be as beneficial as performing the experiment using an animal model. Layla ultimately agreed to participate in the animal experiment, under pressure to comply with the original assignment from her instructor, illustrating that when students are faced with morally controversial practices in their education, they are often easily swayed to align with figures of authority (e.g., Pedersen, 2010; Birke et al., 2007). Similarly, other students who expressed initial hesitation or discomfort to using animals also admitted that they felt compelled to engage in the experiments despite this, citing the pressure they felt by their instructors. Marcus expressed that after conversations with his instructors he realized that animal experimentation is something that you *need* to get used to doing; while Cara stated, "you learn right away of course animals are used all throughout science, so you get accustomed to that." Therefore, even if students do not want to participate in animal experiments, the pedagogy of animal experimentation instills a perceived necessity of this practice in students. Many students also recalled being told that if they wanted to move forward with education and careers in the sciences, most of it would require animal use. Marcus, a prospective medical student, commented that according to his instructors "if you say that you don't want to [use animal models], that really limits your opportunities." Marcus was told this despite the fact that according to the Physicians Committee for Responsible Medicine (PCRM), by 2016, all 202 accredited medical schools in Canada and the United States had removed the use of animals in medical training, switching instead to human-relevant methods (2016). Nonetheless, when students are led to believe that animal use is necessary in order to advance in education and careers in science and medicine, it provides a compelling justification for acceptance based on the potential future repercussions of their opposition.

Understanding students' experiences of animal experimentation and its teaching is extremely important in analyzing how perceptions and experiences are shaped, and how students rationalize this practice as a part of their education. Students' perspectives are developed through their pedagogical exposure, therefore, understanding how they rationalize their engagement in animal experimentation can shed light on the normalization processes used to acclimate students into using animals for experimental purposes, subsequently reproducing animal models as the status quo. As previously suggested, the pedagogy that is taught to students, and the ways that it is presented to them by their instructors, has a significant impact on their perceptions and experiences of animal experimentation in their education. While it is to be expected that instructors and pedagogy influence student perceptions, it becomes problematic when the information being taught is factually misleading and coercively applied to convince students to engage in this practice, especially after they express discomfort. While I attempted to address and engage with student's voices through my interviews, it is apparent that the standard pedagogy in their education acts to marginalize student voice. As noteworthy critical pedagogues and education theorists assert, an unequal power relationship can exist between teachers and students, leading to an imbalance between teacher voice and student voice, in which students are taught to comply with instructors and the educational practices taught to them through a process of pedagogical domination (e.g., Giroux, 1983). Student voice is often marginalized in unequal teacher/student relations, substantiating Freire's concept of the banking model in education, which "transforms students into receiving objects" (2000, p. 77), and imposes a passive role onto them as they are taught to absorb and accept the practices and principles taught to them. This was exhibited in the interviews with students, as they were taught to accept animal experimentation as a necessary part of their education because their instructors told them so. Furthermore, when students did raise their discomfort and concerns to instructors, their voices were dismissed and it was again asserted to them that in order to advance in education and potential careers in research and medicine, animal experimentation was something that they *needed* to do. Therefore, for these students, when they did voice opposition or reservations, their voices were managed and controlled, and through this marginalization of student voice, students were rendered as receiving objects of their instructor's pedagogy.

Just as the subject/object relations in the teacher-student relationship must be challenged and dissolved, so too must the subject/object relations that exist between human-animal relationships in science education. The field of Critical Animal Studies (CAS) developed, in part, to explicitly challenge "Animal Studies (AS), rooted in vivisection and animal testing in the hard sciences" (Nocella II et al., 2014, p. xxiii), is pivotal in achieving this. Central to this field is the premise that animals are agential subjects, thus CAS opposes any and all forms of exploitation, oppression and domination that renders animals as objects for human use (Nocella II et al., 2014). An increasing emphasis on critical pedagogical considerations, in praxis with CAS tenants, has led to Gunnarsson Dinker and Pedersen's introduction of critical animal pedagogies, which invites "scholar-activist educators to examine what education can be if humans are not the center of focus and understood as superior" (Drew et al., 2019, p. 6). As a field, Critical animal pedagogy's (CAP) extension of CAS tenants into pedagogical practice (Repka, 2019), can equip us with the tools to challenge and disrupt speciesist pedagogies that portray animals as "endlessly accessible for human use" (Gunnarsson Dinker & Pedersen, 2019, p. 46). Animal experimentation pedagogy represents perhaps the most overt form of speciesist pedagogy and institutionalized animal violence that exists in formal education, and reinforces a dominative human-animal binary through explicit, null and hidden curriculums. As

Repka (2019) explains, the explicit curriculum (the intended learning objectives and materials taught to students), the hidden curriculum (the implicit unintended values transmitted to students through curriculum, structure and policies), and the null curriculum (the intentionally omitted subjects, disciplines and information) operate conjunctively in ways that often promote anthropocentric and speciesist discourses in education. In context, the promotion of anthropocentric and speciesist discourses through all three types of curriculum were brought to light by the students I spoke with in ways that reinforced their rationalization and perceived necessity of animal models. At the most basic level, the inclusion of animal experimentation as a learning practice in the explicit curriculum teaches students that this practice is acceptable. As Mary explains, "We just assume, 'oh it's school, this is to learn, everything must be fine then'", exemplifying how the mere inclusion of this practice in formal education is enough to teach students that the use of animals in science is ethical and appropriate. The null curriculum is illustrated by student accounts of the intentional omission of non-animal alternatives from courses, which implicitly teaches them that alternatives to animal models are inferior and/or nonexistent. Lastly, under the hidden curriculum, the inclusion of animal models transmits values of human superiority and animal objectification, as learning objectives are prioritized over animal lives. The objectification of animals in pedagogy is both a product and a perpetuation of a speciesist curriculum. As Pedersen (2004) explains, just as a hidden curriculum can convey messages of sexism and racism, it can also contain speciesist elements that impose animal objectification through curriculum and pedagogy. While there is an imperative not to valorize or reward observable racism, sexism, or any other -isms that reinforce oppression and exploitation in education, the same should be true for explicit and implicit speciesism (Schatz, 2019). Under a CAP framework, this must be demanded in order to dispel the subject/object relations that position animals without agency or inherent value.

While some comments from students appeared uncritical of the pedagogical influences in their perceptions of animal experimentation, others were very much cognizant of how their perceptions are actively shaped by pedagogy and their instructors. As Mary reveals "obviously if it's in their [the professor's] class and you're doing experiments on these things, they vouch for it. So, their views are positive, which makes your views positive". Subsequently, Mary also noted that unlike the social science students, who learn about the negative side of animal use and experimentation, in science classes "they only touch on the good stuff." Therefore, Mary acknowledged that her experience of pedagogy only focused on the positive aspects of animal experimentation, which then shaped students' perceptions of this practice as positive. Additionally, Noah and Cara highlighted the vested interests of instructors in valuing animal models because their careers have been built on animal research. Noah asserted that professors surely value the usefulness of this practice "because it does play a major role in their own research." Cara explained that "it's their career" so of course they will teach the necessity of animal use, adding that "they [instructors] do bias us, but not in a bad way ... I think." Thus, students are aware of the potential motives behind their professors' support of animal experimentation in education and research. This is a critical observation, as animal experimentation operates as a part of the animal industrial complex (AIC); a concept coined by Barbara Noske to highlight how animal industries and commodification are embedded in capitalist systems that centralize vested financial interests at the expense of animals, humans and the environment (1997). While data related to the exact amount of funding that is funneled through academic institutions towards animal research and teaching is unavailable, due to the lack of transparency and concealed nature of animal research, Noske (1997) asserts that the existence of this practice in academia is for profit and career-making, as the majority of this animal research is for curiosity and knowledge that has no direct link to human well-being. Additionally, Sorenson (2010) explains that the same is true in Canadian universities, in which animal experimentation means money. Sorenson (2010) illustrates that while the University of British Columbia, a supposed leader in biomedical research, was given lucrative funding to develop a new medical center, the director of that center, Dr. Chris Harvey-Clark, was unable to provide an example of any achieved successes at UBC through animal research. Despite the shortcomings and blatant failings of animal research, universities and faculty are inextricably financially vested in the continuation of animal experimentation (Sorenson, 2010; Noske, 1997), which the explicit, null and hidden curriculums in standard pedagogy help to perpetuate. To this effect, it is unsurprising that non-animal alternatives were marginalized in the educational experiences of my participants, because as Gunnarsson Dinker and Pedersen (2019) explain, "the A-IC relies on the formal education system—from kindergarten to university level—as sites of reproduction of a plethora of animal oppressive practices, conveniently incorporated in the socialization processes of education" (p. 51). In order to reproduce the continued use of animals in research, the use of animal experimentation in education must be understood as an integral part of the AIC, to instill an acceptance and reliance on animal models into the next generation of researchers. Even though students displayed some awareness of these motives, acknowledging the pedagogical bias and coercive tactics in animal experimentation pedagogy, they were largely unbothered by them; they did not confront these issues or look beyond their experiences of pedagogy to challenge them, rather they continued to assert the importance and necessity of animal experimentation, as they've been taught to do.

CONCLUSION

Within the teaching of animal experimentation, instructors influence students through a speciesist pedagogy, and a curriculum that tacitly shapes students' perceptions of animals as research objects and animal experimentation as an essential part of their education. As animal objectification is normalized and embedded throughout education, it can be difficult for students to detect speciesist relations and the value systems behind them (Pedersen, 2004). My current analysis affirms the findings of Birke et al. (2007) and Pedersen (2010), suggesting that students are easily swayed to align with educational authority figures (i.e., instructors), particularly when confronting moral or ethical dilemmas in their education. These findings, coupled with the anthropocentric and speciesist roots embedded in curriculum and pedagogy, have vast implications for human-animal relations in science education and beyond. When envisioning a post-animal era in science research, education and testing, the rejection of anthropocentrism and speciesism embedded in CAP and CAS principles, is crucial in the long-term planning for the replacement of animal models with available non-animal alternatives. As CAP and CAS seek radical and formative shifts in education, and the dismantling of speciesist status quo animal practices and teachings, the disruption of the AIC's lucrative ties to the education system must be challenged and expelled. While students did not believe that non-animal alternatives were advanced enough to be used in replacement of animals at this time, they did agree that if adequate alternatives were available, they would likely preference them over animal models. Therefore, further work under CAP and CAS frameworks is needed to dispel the misconceptions and distrust around non-animal alternative methods, with the ultimate goal of abolishing animal exploitation in science education, and across academic institutions more broadly (Nocella II et al., 2014). Additionally, investigations into sites where alternatives are more prevalently used and encouraged, in order to examine how alternative methods can be expanded in education is necessary. As Canadian post-secondary institutions shift to remote learning in response to the current global COVID-19 pandemic, it would be interesting to explore if and how non-animal alternatives are being incorporated into science curriculum, in lieu of in-person animal experiments, the subsequent educational experiences of students, and how these alternatives can be amplified to replace animal models as the new status quo in education.

REFERENCES

Anderegg, C., Cohen, M. J., Kaufman, S. R., Ruttenberg, R., & Fano, A. (2002). *A critical look at animal experimentation*. Medical Research Modernization Committee.

Arluke, A., & Hafferty, F. (1996). From apprehension to fascination with "dog lab": The use of absolutions by medical students. *Journal of Contemporary Ethnography, 25*(2), 201–225.

Birke, L. (2012). Animal bodies in the production of scientific knowledge: Modelling medicine. *Body & Society,* 18(3 and 4), 156–178.

Birke, L., Arluke, A., & Michael, M. (2007). *The sacrifice: How scientific experiments transform animals and people.* Purdue University Press.

Canadian Council on Animal Care (CCAC). (2020). "CCAC Facts and Figures".https://www.ccac.ca/Documents/Publications/CCAC-Facts-and-Figures.pdf.

Capaldo, T. (2004). The psychological effects on students of using animals in ways that they see as ethically, morally or religiously wrong. *New England Anti-Vivisection Society, 32*(1), 525–531.

Deguchi, B. G., Molento, C. F., & de Souza, C. E. (2012). The perception of students on the use of animals in higher education at the Federal University of Paraná, Southern Brazil. *Alternatives to Laboratory Animals-ATLA, 40*(2), 83.

Drew, C., George, A. E., Ketenci, S., Lupinacci, J., Nocella II, A. J., Purdy, I., & Schatz, J. L. (2019). Introduction: Examining the nexus: Critical animal studies and critical pedagogy. In A. J. Nocella II, C. Drew, A. E. George, S. Ketenci, J. Lupinacci, I. Purdy & J. L. Schatz (Eds.), *Education for total liberation: Critical animal pedagogy and teaching against speciesism* (pp. 1–12). Peter Lang Inc.

Eadie, E. N. (2011). Educational contexts involved in reduction in animal suffering. In *Education for animal welfare* (pp. 37–68). Berlin, Heidelberg: Springer.

Fadali, M. A. (1996). *Animal experimentation: A harvest of shame.* Hidden Springs Press.

Freire, P. (2000). *Pedagogy of the oppressed.* Bloomsbury.

Folescu, R., Miftode, E., & Zamfir, C. L. (2013). Animal experimental studies: Controversies alternatives and perspectives. *Revista de Cercetare si Interventie Sociala, 43,* 266–273.

Giroux, H. A. (1983). *Theory and resistance in education: A pedagogy for the opposition.* Bergin & Garvey.

Greek, R., & Greek, J. (2002). *Specious science: How genetics and evolution reveal why medical research on animals harms humans.* The Continuum International Publishing Group Inc.

Greek, R., & Greek, J. (2010). Is the use of sentient animals in basic research justifiable? *Philosophy, Ethics, and Humanities in Medicine, 5*(14), 1–16.

Gunnarsson Dinker, K., & Pedersen, H. (2019). Critical animal pedagogy: Explorations toward reflective practice. In A. J. Nocella II, C. Drew, A. E. George, S. Ketenci, J. Lupinacci, I. Purdy & J. L. Schatz (Eds.), *Education for total liberation: Critical animal pedagogy and teaching against speciesism* (pp. 45–62). Peter Lang Inc.

Kamat, V. (2014). Fast, cheap, and out of control? Speculations and ethical concerns in the conduct of outsourced clinical trials in India. *Social Science & Medicine, 104,* 48–55.

Lankford, R. D. (2009). *Animal experimentation.* Farmington Hills: Greenhaven Press.

Luke, B. (2007). *Brutal: Manhood and the exploitation of animals.* University of Illinois Press.

Matthews, R. A. J. (2008). Medical progress depends on animal models—Doesn't it? *Journal of the Royal Society of Medicine, 101*(2), 95–98.

Monamy, V. (2009). *Animal experimentation: A guide to the issues.* Cambridge University Press.

Nocella II, A. J., Sorenson, J., Socha, K., & Matsuoka, A. (2014). The emergence of critical animal studies. In A. J. Nocella II, J. Sorenson, K. Socha & A. Matsuoka (Eds.), *Defining critical animal studies: An intersectional social justice approach for liberation* (pp. xix–xxxvi). Peter Lang Inc.

Noske, B. (1997). *Beyond boundaries: Humans and animals.* Black Rose Books.

Nundy, S., & Gulhati, C. M. (2005). A new colonialism?—Conducting clinical trials in India. *New England Journal of Medicine, 352*(16), 1633–1636.

Pedersen, H. (2002). Humane education: Animals and alternatives in laboratory classes: Aspects, attitudes and implications. http://new.interniche.org/system/files/public/conscientious_ob jection/thesis_helena.pdf.

Pedersen, H. (2004). Schools, speciesism, and hidden curricula: The role of critical pedagogy for humane education futures. *Journal of Futures Studies*, *8*(4), 1–14.

Pedersen, H. (2010). *Animals in schools: Processes and strategies in human-animal education.* Purdue University Press.

Physicians Committee for Responsible Medicine. (2016). 31 years of progress: How we replaced animals in medical student training. http://www.pcrm.org/sites/default/files/Medical-Scho ols-Report-2016-2.pdf.

Repka, M. (2019). Intersecting oppressions: The animal industrial complex and theeducational industrial complex. In A. J. Nocella II, C. Drew, A. E. George, S. Ketenci, J. Lupinacci, I. Purdy & J. L. Schatz (Eds.), *Education for total liberation: Critical animal pedagogy and teaching against speciesism* (pp. 99–118). Peter Lang Inc.

Schatz, J. L. (2019). Activist education for animal ethics: The imperative of intervention in education on the non/human. In A. J. Nocella II, C. Drew, A. E. George, S. Ketenci, J. Lupinacci, I. Purdy & J. L. Schatz (Eds.), *Education for total liberation: Critical animal pedagogy and teaching against speciesism* (pp. 155–167). Peter Lang Inc.

Sorenson, J. (2010). *About Canada: Animal rights.* Fernwood Publishing.

Wang, L. (2001). Computer-simulated pharmacology experiments for undergraduate pharmacy-students: Experience from an Australian university. *Indian Journal of Pharmacology*, *33*(4), 280–282.

Waters, J. R., Van Meter, P., Perrotti, W., Drogo, S., & Cyr, R. J. (2011). Human clay models versus cat dissection: How the similarity between the classroom and the exam affects student performance. *Advances in Physiology Education*, *35*(2), 227–236.

CHAPTER FOUR

Nonhuman "Others": A Theology of Hope and Liberation

SARAH TOMASELLO

Religious traditions play a significant role in the way we understand the world around us, and therefore influence our attitudes towards, and interactions with, other species (Waldau, 2006). In Western culture, our society has been largely immersed in the Judeo-Christian tradition, which has had myriad negative implications for nonhuman animals. While there are a number of foundational teachings within Christianity that call for compassionate treatment of all living beings, these are largely ignored in favor of tradition and custom which perpetuate human exceptionalism (Kemmerer, 2012). One theological movement, however, that holds promising teachings for improving our relationship with the more-than-human world is that of liberation theology. Liberation theology is a movement that emerged during the 1960s as both an intellectual and religious response to the poverty, marginalization, and oppression faced by millions of humans across Latin America (Lamb, 1985). It was developed by Latin American communities, together with priests and theologians, calling for a renewal of social justice (Carvalhaes & Fábio, 2017). Christians are called to "see with newly converted eyes," which involves viewing the world from the perspective of the marginalized, as well as taking an active role in solidarity with the oppressed to ensure they do not remain forgotten (Curnow, 2015, p. 33).

Since its inception, this movement has expanded across the globe, encouraging Christians to become actively involved in political and civic affairs in attempt to create a society void of oppressive systems (Rowland, 2008). In the United

States, liberation theology began in the form of Black theology during the civil rights movement, where scholars such as James Cone argued for a connection between Christian ethics and societal transformation (Floyd-Thomas & Pinn, 2010). As Black theology grew and transformed, it inspired other marginalized groups within the United States to organize their own theologies of liberation as a response to their experiences of injustice. This has resulted in Hispanic/Latinx theology, Asian American theology, LGBTQIA theology, feminist theology, American Indian theology, and Environmental/Eco theology, among others (Floyd-Thomas & Pinn, 2010).

Whether the focus on the oppressed and marginalized within the liberation movement could encompass nonhuman animal species, however, has not been made explicitly clear. This is unfortunate, as the goals of liberation theology (including the liberation of the oppressed, rejection of capitalism, and emphasis on intersectionality) are very similar to those of Critical Animal Studies. This chapter, therefore, will examine academic literature in hopes of gaining an understanding of how, if at all, liberation theology has addressed the suffering of nonhuman 'others'. Utilizing Joseph Cardinal Cardijn's See-Judge-Act methodology, along with the core principles of Critical Animal Studies, it will then offer suggestions of ways in which this movement could grow in order to better include nonhuman animals in its scope of concern.

ECO THEOLOGY: A PLACE FOR NONHUMAN 'OTHERS'?

Liberation theology is often described as a new way of doing theology rather than a new theology in and of itself (Rowland, 2008). This is because it directly challenges any concepts within the Christian faith, including understandings of god, Jesus Christ, salvation, and the sacraments, which do not support the liberation of others from systemic injustices (Lamb, 1985). As Carvalhaes and Py (2017) explain, "it is a place where faith, discourse of God, and real life meet in order to protect and expand the possibilities of life, in the ecobiodiversity of the planet and in the possibility of justice for the poor" (p. 157).

Currently, this widening of perspective can be seen in one of the newest movements, ecological theology, which criticizes the anthropocentric nature of previous liberation movements and calls for a theology which deconstructs the human-nature dichotomy (Boff, 2001). There are several characteristics of ecological theology which are extremely useful in improving our relationships with the more-than-human world. Its most central premise is the belief that both the oppression of human beings and the depredation of the environment share a root cause: the culture of profit, greed and power as domination (Boff, 1995). An example of this can be seen when considering industrocentric activities, such as mining, intensive agriculture, and logging, which result not only in the decimation of forest habitat, the pollution of waterways, and the overhunting of wildlife species, but also in the destruction of homes and lifeways of human communities who are intimately connected to their land (Poirier & Tomasello, 2017).

A second, and equally important characteristic of ecological theology, is its critique of subject-object dualisms. These dualisms, such as male/female, rich/poor, culture/nature, are characteristic of "Western" cosmology and are therefore reflected in both our thought and language (McFague, 1997). Christian theology, which is influenced by the subject-object model, gives precedence to the spiritual world over our material world, resulting in lack of appreciation for the Earth and the various forms of life it holds (Haught, 1991). Ecological theology, however, rejects this dualistic and hierarchical way of thinking about the world. Anthropocentrism, it is argued, "reveals a narrow, atomized view of the human being torn away from other beings" (Boff, 2001, p. 74). Since all living beings, and not just humans, were placed on Earth by God, we should instead give emphasis to our interdependence and connectedness to the rest of Creation (Boff, 1995).

While ecological theology has made incredible progress, it unfortunately doesn't go quite far enough to be truly liberating for the more-than-human world. Although it actively denounces anthropocentrism and dualistic thinking, two tenants important within Critical Animal Studies, it has yet to overcome these barriers within its own theological discourse. In its reasoning, living in solidarity with the natural world is not required because this world has intrinsic value in itself, or because the suffering of nonhuman beings is taken as seriously as the suffering of humans, but rather because the degradation of the earth disproportionally impacts humans who suffer from poverty and marginalization. Certainly, God cares about the more-than-human world, and calls us to live together in community, but for many ecological theologians, this is because God wants us to overcome the suffering caused to humans that results from a dominion-based relationship with the Earth. This is illustrated in Leonardo Boff's 1995 article, which argues for the synthesis of liberation theology and ecology. Here, he states:

> The argument is not hard to understand. Either we all save ourselves within a system of living together in solidarity and sharing with and in earth, or we explode it through our indignation and fling us all into the abyss (p. 69).

If the underlying reason we advocate for care of the natural world is because we rely on plants, nonhuman animals, and clean water for our own survival, then ecological theology does not truly free itself of the anthropocentrism that it supposedly rejects.

WIDENING OUR ETHIC OF CARE: ANIMAL LIBERATION

An all-inclusive, life-centered liberation theology must consider the immense amount of suffering faced by nonhuman animals at the hands of humans. While it may seem peculiar for a Christian theology to be so closely aligned with secular animal liberation activism, in reality, liberation theologians and the field of Critical Animal Studies already have much in common.

One of the most notable similarities is their critique of the underlying social structures which maintain injustice. In the book *Terrorists or Freedom Fighters*, Best and Nocella II (2004) explain that animal liberation activism involves working to dismantle the entire institutional framework that allows for the exploitation of nonhumans to occur. Rather than just working to save nonhuman animals from situations where they are suffering, they also work to deconstruct the "domineering values, mindset, identities and worldviews" that lead to this suffering (p. 13). Similarly, liberation theology was founded with the goal of overcoming these systems of oppression that make marginalized humans victims in the first place (Boff, 1995). An example of this is seen in definition of the word "sin," which was expanded by the famous liberation theologian Archbishop Oscar Romero to include social failures, such as racism, classism, sexism, etc., which form into permanent structures exerting power and control over others (Faus, 1993). For both liberation theologians and animal liberationists, dismantling the root cause of oppression is essential to effecting permanent change.

Liberation theology also fits well within Critical Animal Studies with its focus on direct action and its critique of dualistic thinking. Rather than simply discussing liberation in the abstract through academic writings or lectures, liberation theology calls for Christians to be active members in their communities, hearing the voices of the oppressed, and responding directly to those voices (Alanis, 2016). Working collaboratively with those who are marginalized to identify oppressive social structures, and then acting with them to fight for their own liberation is the ultimate goal. As Boff (1995) explains, acting *with*, rather than *for* the oppressed is important, as it acknowledges their agency and critiques the harmful dualism of "savior/in-need-of-saving" (p. 71).

Coming from a secular perspective, Critical Animal Studies has the same core principles. Not only does it promote total liberation activism and direct action, but it also calls activists to listen to and work alongside the oppressed, arguing that non-humans, too, have agency (Nocella II et al., 2014). Like liberation theology, Critical Animal Studies advocates for the deconstruction of dualistic thinking, which results in an "us vs them" mentality and the formation of hierarchies (Boff, 2001).

TOWARDS A MORE-THAN-HUMAN THEOLOGY OF LIBERATION

Inspired by Justin Sands (2018), I will use Joseph Cardinal Cardijn's See-Judge-Act methodology in order to offer a framework for how liberation theology might better include nonhuman animals in its scope of concern. This methodology allows for oppression to be explored in a way that is not abstract, but rather focused on concrete change. This is done by transitioning through a series of phases, beginning with engagement and solidarity, then moving to reflection and understanding, and finally to active collaboration (Sands, 2018).

To develop this framework, I utilize many common themes which run throughout the traditional, anthropocentric liberation theologies, while incorporating the ideas of a number of theologians who are not necessarily labeled as "liberationists", but who are strong advocates of nonhuman animals. These theologians are passionate about the same issues surrounding peace and justice that are characteristic of liberation theologies, both in regard to marginalized humans, but also in terms of our relationship with the Earth and other living beings (Birch et al., 1991). As the realities and perspectives of nonhuman animals are critical to this proposed theology, I also include the voices of anthrozoologists, ecologists, animal rights activists, and ethologists to ensure that we are *seeing, judging*, and *acting* in scientifically informed and responsible ways. It is my hope that this framework will allow these different communities of people to come together in dialogue to create a truly life-centered theology of liberation.

SEEING: AWAKENING FROM OUR ANTHROPOCENTRIC DREAM

To see involves opening one's eyes to how the structures that result in poverty, marginalization, and discrimination against humans are also impacting the nonhuman world. It includes both observing and immersing one's life into the lives of the "other," so as to understand what they are experiencing from their unique point of view (Sands, 2018). Seeing the world through another's eyes is a critical first step if we hope to expand our definition of the moral community and rid ourselves of prejudices against other humans and other species (Best & Nocella II, 2004). We must simultaneously break free from our anthropocentric gaze; see ourselves as a part of Creation, rather than above it, and understand that human qualities and ways of experiencing the world are not normative to others (Sands, 2018).

SEEING OUR CONNECTEDNESS

Perhaps the greatest struggle to seeing the reality of our relatedness to other living beings is anthropocentrism. Many religious traditions, including Christianity, are otherworldly, meaning that they focus on, and give precedence to, the spiritual world over the Earthly world. As a result, we have been made to feel foreign to the natural world around us. The Earth is not considered our true home, but rather a temporary place of dwelling while we wait for salvation and entry into the Kingdom of Heaven. Therefore, it is easy for us to ignore, or at least to not care deeply about, the natural environment and the multitude of nonhuman species that are a part of it (Haught, 1991).

In many ways, ecological theology has already begun to address this issue. Leonardo Boff (2001), for example, refers to the Earth and all living beings as part of a "great cosmic community". Boff explains that because everything is made up of energy, just in differing degrees and levels of stabilization, that all of life is interrelated via "extremely complex systems of relationships" (2001, p. 29). This energy once formed the giant red stars, parts of the Milky Way Galaxy, and the sun, and now makes up each living being today. This reality of connectedness is perhaps most famously expressed within Pope Francis' 2015 encyclical, *Laudato Si'*, where he urges humans to remember that we are the "dust of the earth," as are all living beings, with each of our bodies being comprised of her elements (pp. 3–4). Trees, caterpillars, microorganisms, and humans are not only connected by this underlying "cosmic solidarity," but also depend on one another for their very existence (Francis, 2015, p. 32). Anthropocentrism, therefore, is both illusionary and arrogant (Acosta, 2007; Boff, 2001).

SEEING ANIMAL'S PAIN

As we are learning to see ourselves as intimately connected with Creation, it is also imperative that our eyes are opened to the similarities between humans and other species in our ability to feel physical and emotional pain. Biologically speaking, the emotional and physical suffering faced by humans is similar to that faced by nonhumans. Scientists have concluded that nonhuman species do indeed feel pain, and that this pain is expressed through verbalizations such as cries and squeals, changes in facial expression and gait, aggressiveness, and decrease in appetite, among others (Yarri, 2005). In fact, scientists who study pain have noted that pain physiology and biochemistry are very similar across species (Kitchell & Erickson, 1983), so while there are certainly variances in the way nonhumans experience pain, these are no different than those seen across human cultures or between individual humans (Rollin, 2006).

Furthermore, all mammals, and many non-mammals, share the same neuroanatomical structures necessary for producing emotions, such as the amygdala, hippocampus, and the neurochemical pathways found within the limbic system (Bekoff, 2009, p. 83). Studies have concluded that nonhumans are conscious, meaning they are aware of their environment, their actions, and the actions of those around them, and that they have mental experiences including desires and beliefs, fear, shame, happiness, embarrassment, love, and disgust (Yarri, 2005; Bekoff, 2000). It is clear, then, that what we do to nonhuman animals matters to them (Yarri, 2005), and if we hope to see the realities of the world for what they are, we must take seriously these studies published by biologists, cognitive ethologists, and welfare scientists.

HOW CAN WE BETTER SEE?

Expanding one's vision to better see the realities that other living beings face is no simple task. However, there are a few steps that may help in this journey. The first step, as recommended by theologians Kallistos Ware (2002) and Jay McDaniel (2006), is to spend time observing and quietly contemplating the nonhuman life around you. To observe involves seeing each being in his or her "suchness," looking into their eyes, noticing their different facial expressions, the ways that they move and the sounds they make, and appreciating these unique characteristics (McDaniel, 2006, p. 143). This could be as simple as looking out your window and watching the birds fly to and from branches, observing ants as they march across the sidewalk, or sitting on a park bench and watching the squirrels scurry about. It is much easier to see our connectedness to other creatures when we first take the time to truly notice them.

Seeing the physical and mental suffering of other species can be more difficult, as it often occurs in places where the larger public cannot see. Farms and slaughterhouses are located in the countryside or outskirts of towns, with outside video and photography being strictly prohibited. Additionally, research facilities, more often than not, simply look like any other building and are largely inaccessible to the public. Other forms of violence, such as neglect of, or cruelty towards, companion animals may happen behind the closed doors of people's homes. Still, others are invisible because they are normalized by society, such as the breeding of dogs for specific traits while knowing that these traits result in severe health consequences. In order to see these realities, we must be willing, as well as proactively seek, to educate ourselves on these matters.

Fortunately, there are an endless number of resources available to the public to aid in this task.

JUDGING

Once we have opened our eyes to the realities that nonhuman species endure, we can now begin the process of judging. To judge means to reflect on these various modes of oppression in light of faith and scripture (Sands, 2018). As Leonardo and Clodovis Boff explain, this does not only involve interpreting scripture, but also gaining an understanding of how scripture can be practically applied to better understand, and address, violent and oppressive social structures (Sands, 2018). This section, then, will discuss the ideas of many Christian theologians, ethicists, and philosophers who have already begun this process of judging.

OUR RELATIONSHIP WITH OTHER ANIMALS SHOULD BE REFLECTIVE OF GOD'S LOVE FOR CREATION

When we read and interpret scripture with a life-centered lens as opposed to an anthropocentric lens, it becomes clear that the Bible has much to say about our relationships with the more-than-human world. In fact, theologians such as Andrew Linzey (2009), Lisa Kemmerer (2012), Laura Hobgood- Oster (2010), and J.R. Hyland have devoted entire books arguing for the compassionate treatment of nonhumans from a biblical standpoint. One of the most cited scripture passages that provides a strong foundation for their arguments is the creation story of Genesis 1.Genesis 1 offers two passages in particular that can help guide Christian's relationships with other species. The first is verses 24–25:

> And God said, "Let the earth bring forth living creatures of every kind: cattle and creeping things and wild animals of the earth of every kind." And it was so. God made the wild animals of the earth of every kind, and the cattle of every kind, and everything that creeps upon the ground of every kind. And God saw that it was good (NRSV).

Reflecting on this passage, Himes and Himes (1990) explain that nonhuman animals exist because of God's grace, creativity, and love. Since these species were created before humans and were deemed to be good independently from them, this suggests that they have intrinsic value and were not made for the purpose of exploitation (Webb, 1998). Albert Schweitzer expands upon this view in his theology of 'Reverence for Life'. He argues that each species, and each individual within a species, has importance in and of itself, and that each has a role to play within the universe. As humans stuck in our own subjective realities, we could not possibly assume that we know God's plan for each of these beings (Daly, 1991)

This being said, we must stop creating hierarchies by judging nonhuman others in relation to ourselves and then treating those who are not "close enough" to us as if they only have instrumental value (Nocella II et al., 2014; Daly, 1991, p. 99). If God deemed all of Creation as 'good,' this means God places value on all nonhuman beings, not only companion animals or charismatic megafauna, but also those species which we exploit for food, and those which we kill out of fear and disgust (Yarri, 2005).

FOSTERING A "SACRAMENTAL CONSCIOUSNESS"

A second way in which humans can begin to judge the treatment of non-human 'others' is through the principle of sacramentality. In the Roman Catholic tradition, a sacrament is that which embodies the divine grace, love and gift that is God (Himes & Himes, 1990). Because God created the world entirely out of an act of love, all of creation can be seen as a sacrament of God's goodness and creativity (Himes & Himes, 1990). The concept of sacramentality, then, is seeing all living beings as being reflective of God's self, and therefore as an opportunity to be in the presence of God (Berry, 1991). This means that all beings, whether they be plant, nonhuman animal, or human, have an element of holiness within them (Habgood, 1991).

A sacramental view of the world teaches us that one of the best ways to connect with the divine is by seeing and interacting with the more-than-human world around us. While eco-theologians tend to apply this concept to the natural world in general, it can also be used to specifically guide our relationships with non-human animal species. If God is present in the hen forced into the battery cage, the fox caught in a leg-hold trap, or the pelican whose belly is full of plastic, we are not only disrespecting the Creation that God so clearly values, but we are also losing ways of learning about and experiencing God as we cause these beings to suffer and die (Habgood, 1991).

TRANSFORMATIVE ACTION: CREATING A NON-HIERARCHICAL, LIFE-CENTERED, THEOLOGY

As Leonardo and Clodovis Boff explain, "at the end of the day, liberation theology leads to action: action for justice, the work of love, conversion, renewal of the church, and the transformation of society" (Sands, 2018, p. 6). Once one participates in the task of seeing and judging, they may then work to develop a series of actions that offer concrete solutions to the suffering faced by nonhuman animal species. This is by no means a simple task. While traditional liberation theology advocates for the "working-with" approach, empowering those who are marginalized and allowing them to take charge of their own liberation, a liberation theology for nonhumans, unfortunately, must follow a different route. Due to limitations in our ability to communicate effectively with other species, theologians must work in solidarity with ethologists, biologists, and anthrozoologists to ensure that each action taken is in the best interest of each unique species. Their knowledge of species-specific behaviors are essential so that the "liberator" does not mistakenly turn into the oppressor (Sands, 2018). Transformative action may therefore take many forms depending on the species and the mode of oppression inflicted upon that species.

The next section provides a number of ideas for actions that can be taken by liberation theologians to directly relieve the suffering of nonhumans and work towards deconstructing the oppressive social structures which objectify them.

ACTING NEIGHBORLY

In his essay, *Christian Obligation for the Liberation of Nature*, Charles Birch (1991) suggests that humans must "seek to be neighbourly" to the nonhumans we share the earth with (p. 65). To be neighborly means to make adequate space for other species within our communities, to ensure that their needs are being met, and to try to remove anything that might be causing their suffering (Birch, 1991). This is a very useful foundation to help us consider actions that can be taken directly in the communities in which we live. These may take the form of reconciliation ecology projects, partnerships with a local "farm-animal" sanctuary, or collaborations with animal liberation groups to remove nonhumans from abusive and exploitative situations.

As the name suggests, reconciliation ecology is the process of reconciling our relationship with the more-than-human world around us by establishing and maintaining new wildlife habitats in the very places where humans live and work (Warners et al., 2014). It calls on us to reconsider the ways in which we are interacting with our surrounding landscape so that the nonhuman animal species who also rely on this landscape are able to flourish. What makes this especially useful for a life-centered theology of liberation is that it stresses that humans are an integral part of Creation. Rather than supporting the human-nonhuman dichotomy by creating separate "natural" spaces for wildlife species, reconciliation ecology challenges us to live in ways that support the species whom are a part of our communities (Warners et al., 2014).

Reconciliation projects can vary greatly depending on the species one is focusing on, and the type of community one lives in (e.g. rural, urban, or suburban).

Therefore, it is important that research is done during the "seeing" phase to identify any features within one's community that might be directly harming wildlife, which species are struggling the most, and what their specific needs are. After determining the species and their needs, Christians can be leaders within their communities for ensuring these needs are being met. Community projects might include the transformation of backyards into wildlife habitats and the creation of corridors between yards to allow for movement. Hosting educational workshops in churches or community centers would be essential so that individuals can learn about which native plant species they should utilize, the importance of eliminating pesticide use, and ways to incorporate elements such as logs, pools of water, bird nesting boxes, and bat houses.

Our communities are comprised of more than just wildlife species, they also include the companion animals that we share our homes with, and the domesticated species whom are subjugated to provide humans with food and clothing. To 'act neighborly', then, must be extended to these living beings as well. One way in which liberation theology can accomplish this is by encouraging partnerships with local shelters and sanctuaries whereby members of a faith community come together on a bi-weekly basis to volunteer. This might entail cleaning cages, barns, or litter boxes, grooming horses, walking dogs, socializing cats, or event planning/administrative work. Not only would this be a direct act of caring for the abandoned, neglected and abused members of God's Creation, but it would also help those who are volunteering to learn more about these nonhumans as individual beings and see better the reality of their suffering.

The final, and most radical neighborly action Christians can take is to work directly with secular animal liberation groups, organizing and participating in protests, sit-ins, and other acts of civil disobedience. While this can be more complicated than working on habitat restoration projects or volunteering at sanctuaries, as Nocella II et al. (2015) explain, it is essential work that brings attention and awareness to modes of exploitation and helps to dismantle them. Not surprisingly, liberation theology itself actually has a rich history of protest and civil disobedience, it simply needs to expand its scope of concern to include the oppression of non-human others in order to be the truly intersectional movement it hopes to be (Boff, 2001).

OVERCOMING OUR "ARROGANT EYE"

Taking action to overcome our anthropocentric view of the world is perhaps the trickiest step, as it requires us to actively change deeply engrained cultural attitudes and societal norms regarding other species. However, it is also one of the most important steps because these attitudes directly influence our behaviors, therefore determining the way we interact with the more-than-human world around us (Manfredo, 2008). The field of Conservation Psychology has contributed much research on this topic, and therefore offers some excellent ideas which Christians can use to transition from an "arrogant gaze" to one that is loving, appreciative, and humble (McFague, 1997). One issue in particular that this field offers advice on is how to help overcome attitudes of fear and disgust that humans have towards certain animal species. This is an important issue because when humans are fearful or disgusted by another species, they may react harshly (consider, for example, ant poison, mouse traps, and wasp spray). Not only does this cause these individuals pain and suffering, but it also prevents them from preforming their roles in processes like pollination and nutrient cycling.

Innumerable studies show that humans are much more open to and tolerable of species after they gain an understanding of that species' biology and the ecological importance that they boast (Jacobson et al., 2006; Johansson & Karlsson, 2011). For example, a study conducted by Randler et al. (2012) found that educational programs which taught children about the biology of disgust-inducing species, and allowed the children to interact with them, resulted in a positive shift in their attitudes towards, and interest in, these various species. With this in mind, Christian communities could partner with local organizations, such as nature preserves, wildlife sanctuaries, and centers for environmental education, to help foster awareness of these species.

TRANSITIONING TO, AND PROMOTING A SIMPLER, WASTE-FREE LIFESTYLE

Given the damage that nonhuman animals are subjected to is a result of our neoliberal, consumer-based culture, a final action that Christians can take is to reject capitalism, and transition into a life-conscious lifestyle. Such a lifestyle has three main features. First, it is minimalist, meaning one makes an effort to reduce their belongings to only things which they truly love or need. Things they no longer need can be donated or upcycled, and a commitment is made to make thoughtful purchases in the future. Entangled within this is the second feature: developing responsible buying habits. This means that when one is buying something that one needs, they choose products that were produced in ethical ways. This might include choosing products that have not been tested on animals, that are Rainforest Alliance certified (if appropriate), and that are fairly traded with the human communities that produce them. The final component of this lifestyle is that it is low-waste, meaning efforts are made to reduce reliance on non-recyclable products that end up polluting the homes of wildlife species. Utilizing glass or metal containers to store food, carrying a reusable water bottle, and learning to make your own cleaning supplies with common household ingredients are all examples of steps that can be taken to reduce the amount of waste one is creating.

CONCLUDING REMARKS

Reflecting on what has been presented in these previous sections can be overwhelming, as the institutional violence towards nonhuman animals is a complex issue and cannot be solved by any one action or process alone. In fact, there are far more modes of oppression, as well as options of addressing them, than this chapter could hope to cover. However, liberation theology, in conjunction with Critical Animal Studies, is very well suited to take on this challenge due to its radical option for the poor, criticism of socially constructed hierarchies, rejection of capitalism, and insistence on action. Theologians must reflect further upon these issues, utilizing the phase of 'seeing' for themselves so that they may better guide Christians in their relationships with the more-than-human world around them. In order for this life-centered theology to grow and adapt, theologians must also work alongside ecologists, wildlife biologists, welfarists, and animal rights activists in order to share knowledge and encourage the birth of new ideas. Creating a truly life-centered theology of liberation, which takes action against all forms of institutional violence, both human and nonhuman alike, will require a concerted interdisciplinary effort.

REFERENCES

Acosta, J. (2007). A theology for another possible world is possible. In M. Althaus-Reid, I. Petrella & L. Susin (Eds.), *Another possible world: Reclaiming liberation theology* (pp. 178–193). CSM Press.

Alanis, J. (2016). Peace and liberation theology. *Global Virtue Ethics Review, 7*(3), 34–43.

Bekoff, M. (2000). Animal emotions: Exploring passionate natures: Current interdisciplinary research provides compelling evidence that many animals experience such emotions as joy, fear, love, despair, and grief—we are not alone, *BioScience, 50*(10), 861–870.

Bekoff, M. (2009). Animal emotions, wild justice and why they matter: Grieving magpies, a pissy baboon, and empathic elephants. *Emotion, Space and Society, 2*(2), 82–85.

Berry, T. (1991). The spirituality of the Earth. In C. Birch, W. Eakin, & J. McDaniel (Eds.), *Liberating life: Contemporary approaches to ecological theology* (pp. 151–158). Orbis Books.

Best, S., & Nocella II, A. (Eds.). (2004). *Terrorists or freedom fighters? Reflections on the liberation of animals.* Lanturn Books.

Birch, L. Charles. (1991). Christian obligation for the liberation of nature. In C. Birch, W. Eaken, & J. B. McDaniel (Eds.), Liberating life: Contemporary approaches in ecological theology (pp. 57-71). Orbis Books.

Birch, C., Eakin, W., & McDaniel, J. (1991). Introduction. In C. Birch, W. Eakin, & J. McDaniel (Eds.), *Liberating life: Contemporary approaches to ecological theology* (pp. 1–5). Orbis Books.

Boff, L. (1995). Liberation theology and ecology: Alternative, confrontation or complementarity. *International Journal for Theology, 5*, 67–77

Boff, L. (2001). *Cry of the Earth, cry of the poor* (P. Berryman, Trans.). Orbis Books.

Carvalhaes, C., & Py, F. (2017). Liberation theology in brazil: Some history, names and themes. *Cross Currents, 67*(1), 157.

Curnow, R. M. (2015). Which preferential option for the poor? A history of the doctrine's bifurcation. *Modern Theology, 31*(1), 27–59.

Daly, L. (1991). Ecofeminism, reverence for life, and feminist theological ethics. In C. Birch, W. Eakin, & J. McDaniel (Eds.), *Liberating life: Contemporary approaches to ecological theology* (pp. 57–71). Orbis Books.

Faus, J. I. G. (1993). Anthropology: The person and the community. In I. Ellacuria & J. Sobrino (Eds.), *Sin in mysterium liberationis: Fundamental concepts of liberation theology* (pp. 532-542). Orbis Books.

Francis, P. (2015). *Laudato si: On care for our common home.* Our Sunday Visitor.

Floyd-Thomas, S. M., & Pinn, A.B. (2010). *Liberation theologies in the united states: An introduction.* New York University Press.

Habgood, John. (1991). A sacramental approach to environmental issues. In C. Birch, W. Eakin, & J. McDaniel (Eds.), *Liberating life: Contemporary approaches to ecological theology* (pp. 27–36). Orbis Books.

Haught, John F. (1991). Religious and cosmic homelessness: Some environmental implications. In C. Birch, W. Eakin, & J. McDaniel (Eds.), *Liberating life: Contemporary approaches to ecological theology* (pp. 159–181). Orbis Books.

Himes, M., & Himes, K. (1990). The sacrament of creation: Toward an environmental theology. *Commonweal, 117*(2), pp. 42-43.

Hobgood-Oster, L. (2010). *The friends we keep: Unleashing Christianity's compassion for animals.* Baylor University Press.

Jacobson, S. K., McDuff, M. D., & Monroe, M. C. (2006). *Conservation education and outreach techniques.* Oxford University Press.

Johansson, M. & Karlsson, J. (2011). Subjective experience of fear and the cognitive interpretation of large carnvores. *Human Dimensions of Wildlife, 16*(1), 15-29.

Kemmerer, L. (2012). *Animals and world religions.* Oxford University Press.

Kitchell, R. L., & Eickson, H. H. (1983). *Animal pain: Perception and alleviation.* Oxford University Press.

Lamb, M. L. (1985). Liberation theology and social justice. *Process Studies, 14*(2), 102–122.

Linzey, A. (2009). *Creatures of the same god: Explorations in animal theology.* Lantern Books.

Manfredo, M. J. (2008). *Who cares about wildlife?* Springer.

McDaniel, J. B. (2006). Practicing the presence of god: A Christian approach to animals. In P. Waldau & K. Patton (Eds.), *A Communion of subjects: Animals in religion, science, and ethics* (pp. 132–145). Columbia University Press.

McFague, S. (1997). The loving eye vs the arrogant eye. *The Ecumenical Review, 49*(2), 185–193.

Nocella II, A. J., Sorenson, J., Socha, K., & Matsuoka, A. (Eds.). (2014). *Defining critical animal studies. An intersectional social justice approach for liberation.* Peter Lang Inc.

Nocella II, A. J., White, R., & Cudworth, E. (Eds.). (2015). *Anarchism and animal liberation. Essays on complementary elements of total liberation.* McFarland & Company Inc.

Poirier, N., & Tomasello, S. (2017). Polar similar: Intersections of anthropology and conservation. *Animalia, 3*(1), 1–20.

Randler, C., Hummel, E., & Prokop, P. (2012). Practical work at school reduces disgust and fear of unpopular animals. *Society & Animals, 20*(1), 61–74.

Rollin, B. (2006). *Science and ethics.* Cambridge University Press.

Rowland, C. (2008). *The cambridge companion to liberation theology.* Cambridge University Press.

Sands, J. (2018). Introducing cardinal Cardin's see–judge–act as an interdisciplinary method to move theory into practice. *Religions, 9*(4), 1–10.

Waldau, P. (2006). Seeing the terrain we walk: Features of the contemporary landscape of "Religion and animals." In P. Waldau & K. Patton (Eds.). *A communion of subjects: Animals in religion, science, and ethics* (pp. 40–57). Columbia University Press.

Ware, K. (2002). *The orthodox way.* St. Vladimir's Seminary Press.

Warners, D., Ryskamp, M., & Van Dragt, R. (2014). Reconciliation ecology: A new paradigm for advancing creation care. *Perspectives on Science and Christian Faith, 66*(4), 221.

Webb, S. H. (1998). *On god and dogs: A Christian theology of compassion for animals.* Oxford University Press.

Yarri, D. (2005). *The ethics of animal experimentation: A critical analysis and constructive Christian proposal.* Oxford University Press.

CHAPTER FIVE

The V-Stamp as an Indirect Crime Against the Animals

ANNIE BERNATCHEZ

In April 2020 I had to face the harsh reality of companion animal veterinarians. My 16-year-old friend M. Charles got sick. That month, many veterinarians ran tests on him and tried to figure out the source of the sickness. Nothing. No diagnosis, no remedy, and no cure. The prospect of euthanasia dragged me into despair and disbelief at the idea of losing my friend; $3000 was not enough to heal his feline body. By the end of that month, my tears and love for him drove us to my mom's place; he had to be hugged by her loving arms and felt the crisp and soft grass of spring under his paws before a heartbreaking adieu. As mysterious as the sickness, his walk on the lawn and some advice from my mom put him, though slowly, on the mend. As M. Charles was recovering, my 18-year-old friend Minette was enjoying my last kisses and cuddles. A year before she had been diagnosed with kidney failure. Subcutaneous fluid helped her to keep going through the disease but this time the symptoms were indicating something other than dehydration and a high level of toxins in her body. On the last day, I was told she likely had a lung tumor and even with the medications that were given to her I had to tell her, one last time, how much I loved her and how grateful I was to have met her. I held her tight against my heart. What was an ill but lively body had become a little fur ball that was about to become sad and lovely memories. That day, $900 was spent in veterinary fees including the purchase of her death.

These two devastating stories made me realize how life and death have a subjective price and how the veterinary profession is pervaded with speciesism, capitalism, and to some extent, by a lack of empathy. There are many veterinarians who truly care for animals and use their expertise in their best interest; they are not the focus of this essay. Needless to say, charging outrageous fees is not a violent crime against the animals but crime has many shades. It is common to blame governmental subsidies and direct animal exploiters like farm and laboratory workers insofar as they normalize the use and abuse of animals' bodies for food, clothes, material, and scientific fantasies. Animal exploitation is institutionalized through practices that use and abuse animals' bodies as commodities. Some animals are categorized as food and/or scientific material, and members of the veterinary profession participate in this oppressive categorization through the approval and regulation of animal welfare policies and guidelines.

Although some veterinarians directly participate in animal abuse, this essay focuses on indirect participation in what should be considered as crimes against animals by administrative veterinarians who have the legitimacy to engage in delusive policies and guidelines promoting animal welfare in farms and laboratories. As their expertise stamp is socially authoritative, administrative veterinarians collaborate with animal industries and governmental authorities to establish an acceptable level of animal abuse. In doing so, exploitation is normalized. Thus, a "V-Stamp" is a marker of the regulation of institutionalized human interference on animals' bodies by administrative veterinarians who legitimize exploitation through animal welfare. By investigating how the veterinary profession contributes to violent crimes against farm and laboratory animals, I explore the question of the role of administrative veterinarians as they participate in the regulation of animal use and abuse through a Critical Animal Studies (CAS) perspective. CAS is anti-speciesist, intersectional and advocates for the abolition of animal exploitation through a total liberation standpoint (Nocella II et al., 2014; Nocella II et al., 2015). Therefore, this essay has a political agenda of initiating a discussion on the role of administrative veterinarians in animal exploitation and holding them accountable for participating in what *should be considered as* crimes against animals kept in farms and laboratories.

THE VETERINARY PROFESSION AS LEGITIMATE EXPERTISE FOR ANIMAL EXPLOITATION

As a member of the veterinary medical profession, I solemnly swear that I will use my scientific knowledge and skills for the benefit of society. I will strive to: promote animal health and welfare, prevent and relieve animal suffering, protect the health of the public and the environment, and advance comparative medical knowledge. I will perform my professional duties conscientiously, with dignity, and in keeping with the principles of veterinary medical ethics. I will strive continuously to improve my professional knowledge and competence and to maintain the highest professional and ethical standards for myself and the profession.

The veterinary oath of the Canadian Veterinary Medical Association (CVMA) is the essence of the profession. The first sentence highlights its speciesist centerpiece. Most people would think veterinarians care for the animals as they are experts of animals' bodies in terms of suffering, diseases, health, and well-being. Consequently, it may be shocking to find out that veterinarians vow to use their expertise for the sake of *human* society. Such authority towards and responsibility for animals can easily be tailored for capitalist purposes by speciesist and disengaged veterinarians as it has been identified among various professions working with the animal industrial complex (Nocella II et al., 2015; Nocella II & George, 2019). Government and research veterinarians, or administrative veterinarians, are experts of animal use and abuse. Their expertise is key to regulating animal exploitation in farms and laboratories. Administrative veterinarians are closely tied to the industry that they contribute to regulate; they have the institutional authority to define what is acceptable animal use and abuse, and provide ethical cover for cruel activities when analyzed from a critical perspective of total liberation.

A survey by the Canadian Veterinary Medical Association (2018) of its members recorded about 13,000 veterinarians: 75% work in private practice, 10% for government, 6% for veterinary industries, 5% in the fields of teaching and research, and 4% in other fields. Government and research veterinarians participate in developing policies and guidelines for animal welfare. They are inspectors in food processing facilities and/or in charge of animal health programs as well as advisors for government policies. In addition, veterinarians in research institutions self-regulate their own mode of exploitation as they determine the emotional and physical level of animal abuse. These two categories refer to administrative veterinarians who are discussed in this chapter as their expertise legitimates animal abuse in farms and laboratories, which should be considered as indirectly criminal.

Health Canada, which has control over human food consumption, is the authority under which the Canadian Food Inspection Agency (CFIA) safeguards animals commodified as food. The CFIA is associated with various veterinary organizations and policies that vouch for animal health and welfare. For instance, the Health of Animals Act and the Health of Animals Regulations are both administrative procedures aimed at ameliorating animal exploitation with an economic twist, maximizing profits from animals' bodies. In addition to federal Acts, Canadian provinces and territories have their own legislation on how to exploit animals kept on farms (Government of Canada, 2014). Although the interference with animals' bodies is regulated by legitimate authorities, exploitation of silenced bodies is left to a cultural perception of suffering and usage.

The CFIA's Chief Veterinary Officer (CVO) has the power to regulate animal health as well as to give strategic and scientific advice to authorities such as the federal Minister of Agriculture. This regulation covers some dimensions of exploitation such as biosecurity, import and export, traceability, diseases, transportation, hatcheries, and slaughter. Every bodily interference on animals has a detailed protocol and a speciesist terminology that depict animals as mere commodities for human consumption. Furthermore, the CVO is one of many CVMA stakeholders that engage in the animal welfare stamp for animal profiteers. Another stakeholder is the National Farmed Animal Health and Welfare Council, where one co-chair is a pig and dairy farmer while the other is a veterinarian and prior CVO for the province of Quebec. The elaborate affiliation between farm animal profiteers and administrative veterinarians is a blatant capitalistic network in which animals are the fulcrum of speciesist exploitation but, conversely, are also silenced and hidden commodities.

In the scientific field, authorities like the Canadian Council on Animal Care (2020) participate in the regulation of animal testing. The network of testing and vivisection supporters has advanced a policy of welfare for animal-based science, the Three Rs policy. The three Rs stand for "Replacement" (avoiding and/or replacing animals), "Reduction" (reducing the number of animals used), and "Refinement" (modifying procedures to minimize pain and distress). Such an "ethical policy" has the effect of maintaining animal exploitation in a more invisible way, albeit less questioned, instead of abolishing the use and abuse of animals; it shows that animal profiteers are able to self-regulate their own abusive activities for idealistic goals and financial interests. In addition to a network of veterinarians who participate in policies and procedures in science, there is a group called the Canadian Association for Laboratory Animal Medicine that justifies the interests of vivisection defenders. Yet, the Canadian Animal Health Institute is an organization that distributes animal health products (e.g., medication, feed additives, animal pesticides) for animals categorized as livestock. In 2018, the profit in this sector was approximately $860 million (Canadian Animal Health Institute, 2020). Policies and guidelines of animal welfare for scientific agendas induce some peace of mind for animal profiteers and the general public at the expense of abused animals' bodies. Such associations of veterinary institutions are hugely profitable, which is evidence that the V-Stamp is capitalist and that exploitation and torture of animals will inevitably happen to turn a profit.

STRUCTURAL ARRANGEMENTS FOR A LEGITIMATE V-STAMP

Animal exploitation in the food and testing industries is seen as a normal component of the current cultural and economic system. Such use and abuse of animals' bodies entail cruelty and torture that goes far beyond what most people would imagine. As defined by Agnew (1998, p. 179), animal abuse is "any act that contributes to the pain or death of an animal or that otherwise threatens the welfare of an animal." He adds, "Such abuse may be physical (including sexual) or mental, may involve active maltreatment or passive neglect, may be direct or indirect, intentional or unintentional, socially approved or condemned, and/or necessary or unnecessary (however defined)" (p. 179). Agnew's definition of abuse obliges to consider the V-Stamp as an indirect crime towards the animals as it guarantees harm to animals as a result. As video footage obtained from undercover and open animal rights and liberation investigators reveals, animal profiteers who interfere with farm and laboratory animals' bodies induces evident physical and mental suffering. Nonetheless, legitimate regulation of the exploitation of animals' bodies needs a culture of speciesism that normalizes crimes amid exploitation for financial interests.

THE CULTURE OF SPECIESISM

Human superiority over other animal species is consistently seen across societies. For instance, the Western world has inherited religious values through which an anthropocentric perspective has set the table for systemic oppression towards animals. As explained by Ryder (2000), speciesism refers to moral considerations that discriminates against animals based on species membership. The speciesist legacy has its roots in ancient Christianity which posits an anthropocentric and hierarchical attitude and perception of the human position on Earth. Such a mindset continued to be dominant through the Renaissance and Enlightenment epochs, which we have inherited today. When the Scientific Revolution occurred, René Descartes laid down the foundations of justified animal exploitation through what we know as science. From then on, animals have become machines and have been perceived as being devoid of both reason and emotion. Said to be unable to think and rationalize, and much less capable to feel pain, animals have been set up for years of appalling torture to fuel scientific fantasies.

The scientific ideal is an additional oppressive layer supporting the superiority of humankind. The assertion that animals do not feel pain and have no capacity for cognition was and still is key to constructs made by the agribusiness and scientific communities which enable the use and abuse of animals' bodies. In fact, it is through advantageous social constructs for humans that animals become objectified. Although there remains a deep controversy about animal suffering, anyone would agree that someone who screams and writhes while beaten or cut is in pain. Moreover, many ethologists have testified that animals do have emotions (Bateson, 2011; de Waal, 2011). Religion and science are both cultural components of speciesism that permit animal exploitation.

Culture is a shared understanding of the world—emotion, morality, and cognition—and their embodiments (Jasper, 1997, p. 44). When speciesism is addressed as a cultural component of societies, it means that shared meaning and knowledge about human and nonhuman animals as well as representations of animals are based on discrimination and injustice. As humans are born into a speciesist culture, they experience a world that orders and normalizes human supremacy over other animal species. According to Schütz (1999, p. 72), cultural legacies can be considered as a "stock of knowledge" by which he meant "the intersubjective world which existed long before our birth, experienced and interpreted by others, our predecessors, as an organized world." It is through a speciesist stock of knowledge that veterinarians experience and interpret their role as animal experts. But speciesist knowledge is also a condition for the commodification of animals.

ANIMALS IN THE TURMOIL OF CAPITALISM

Capitalism is a form of political economy in which animals' bodies are objectified as private property to be transformed into everyday products and distributed as commodities. The commodification of animals for food or scientific fantasies is an essential but criminal feature of the current economic system. As Marx (2011 [1867]) explained, a commodity is an object produced through labor with a useful purpose for humankind. A commodity has a value and can be exchanged on the market. The current Western economic perspective deems animals' bodies as merchandise that can be bred, bought, used, sold, and slaughtered or discarded depending on the value of the species and interspecies lineage. The value of animals' bodies as commodities varies depending on the circumstances and what is being valued and how. For instance, a dog has greater value than a pig as a companion animal, but the reverse is true for food. In Western societies, companion animals are generally more highly valued than "food" animals but still vivisectionists prefer torturing beagle dogs as they are more docile. The objectification of animals' bodies derives from a stock of knowledge that is convenient for animal profiteers who surmise that the pain of animals is not morally important nor that they have personal interests in life. Hence, capitalism has uplifted the dematerialization of animals as living beings while commodifying their bodies through market valuation, which has resulted in the living but lifeless dimension of animal existence.

Although slaughtered animals' bodies reintroduce the "life" behind various products, the value of commodities is strongly associated to the status of what was once a living being. Before the physical transformation from a live body into merchandise, animals involuntarily take part in a "labor of paws." It is for Haraway

(2007) the lively dimension of commodities such as dogs who are attributed various exploitative usages like serving someone. It is fair to say that hens, pigs, monkeys, horses, and mice, just to name a few exploited species, are lively commodities before being socially reintroduced as slaughtered and transformed commodities. Farm animals are both lively and lifeless commodities, while it is more common for laboratory animals to only be a lively commodity as their tormented bodies are discarded. The complexity of political economic relations between human desires and lively versus lifeless commodities is ordered by the rules of capitalism. Hence, administrative veterinarians perform animal "welfare" functions for economic purposes while speciesism legitimates the V-Stamp (and vice versa). Operating within such an understanding of the world are the administrative veterinarians who perform their role as experts of what should be considered as violent crimes against animals.

SOCIO-PSYCHOLOGICAL CONDITIONS AND CONSEQUENCES OF CARING PROFESSIONS

Administrative veterinarians have the legitimate(d) power to participate in the regulation of the use and abuse of animals' bodies in institutions where exploitation takes place. As experts whose stamp is shaped by ingrained speciesism and capitalism, socio-psychological aspects of the profession as trauma work must not be overlooked but rather closely examined to further understand the conditions of the V-Stamp. In that respect, work on the moral disengagement towards animal exploitation and the empathy-based stress of caring professions such as veterinary work can be instructive.

MORAL DISENGAGEMENT AS A KEY SOCIO-PSYCHOLOGICAL CONDITION

As argued in this essay, legal interferences on animals' bodies should be considered as violent crimes against animals, but instead they are normalized and supported through welfare guidelines created and followed by experts whose practices are protected. These harmful practices are legally justified ways of hurting animals for no legitimate reason. From a CAS perspective, this is unacceptable as it subjugates animals instead of liberating them. In the context of animal exploitation, moral disengagement is a self-reflective process to justify grievous actions towards animal species (Mitchell, 2011). Speciesist justification for exploiting animals is also to be found in the narrative of science when testing on animals is undertaken in the name of "scientific knowledge." This is reminiscent of some religious practices like animal sacrifice for spiritual beliefs. In any case, disengagement from moral actions towards animals has been beneficial for understanding various dimensions of human-animal relationships: acceptability of violence (Mitchell, 2011; Vollum et al., 2004), science (DuBois et al., 2016), the meat paradox (Buttlar & Walther, 2019; Graça et al., 2016), and mental health of protection administrators (Wu, 2020). The moral agency of disengagement towards animals provides a conditional socio-psychological basis to understanding the V-Stamp as animal exploitation.

As explained by Mitchell (2011), ordinary people supporting the farming industries—while also opposing animal abuses—are morally disengaged towards animals. In fact, most people comply with and support animal exploitation for food consumption on the grounds of the farming industry principles: "consumers do not actually have to do anything violent or abusive themselves but only have to support an industry that does it on their behalf" (Mitchell, 2011, p. 53). This means that participating in crimes against animals is more often indirect. One does not need to directly torture or murder an animal to be involved in their violent abuse. Indirectly supporting farming also plays a key role in sustaining animal exploitation. Without indirect participation, the farming industry would collapse as would the experimentation industry. Thus, Mitchell draws attention to how the acquiescence towards violent crimes in farming canalizes the speciesist and capitalistic system of animal exploitation enabling moral disengagement.

Mitchell (2011) identifies six conditions particular to the farming industry that are key components to the moral permissibility of animal exploitation. First, "positive roles" are legitimate and meaningful social positions that espouse cultural meaning and are portrayed in media as essential to society, for instance, farmers, slaughter truck drivers, butchers, and veterinarians. Second, the farming industry needs "societal channels for action and basic rules" to lawfully exploit animals (e.g., financial incentives and legislation for abuse). Powerful businesses and government boards need such a logical system of legal abuse to secure financial interests. A third condition is hierarchical thinking essential to "justification and advantageous comparison." Indeed, human supremacy is essential to justifying the farming of animals as they must be considered "as lesser beings who are being rightfully used for the purposes for which they are believed to exist" (Mitchell, 2011, p. 47). Another condition for moral disengagement towards farm animals is the maintenance of a "physical and psychological distance" of what is going on in farms and slaughterhouses. Isolating those premises benefits the farming industry as it can then misrepresent its animal exploitation. A fifth condition is the linguistic aspect that assists prejudicial discourse through the manipulation of language. For instance, meat is never referred to as flesh from a slaughtered animal, and "packing plant" sounds better than murder or killing facilities. Such semantics are euphemisms that aim to curtail one's emotion and ethics vis-à-vis violent abuses. The last condition identified by Mitchell is the "deindividuation" of animals. Farm animals are anonymized—usually they have a number instead of a name—to perpetuate an objectified status of seeing animals as commodities. Such deindividuation normalizes animal exploitation by dissolving the responsibility for animal abuse. Although Mitchell explains moral disengagement of ordinary people towards farm animals, the rationale is apropos for laboratory animals and also morally disengaged administrative veterinarians.

EMPATHY-BASED STRESS AS A CONSEQUENCE OF TRAUMA WORK

As stated by Perret (2020, p. 10), it "is reasonable to assume that veterinarian mental health may impact veterinary recipients of care in a similar manner to those of human medical care." Based on a CVMA survey in 2012, the only available data at the time, Perret found that the majority (51%) of veterinarians had experienced burnout. Furthermore, veterinarians also undergo anxiety, depression, and emotional exhaustion. Perret's research suggests that situations of poor mental health of veterinarians in Canada may also impact their work.

More studies have also drawn attention to the psychological struggle of working with animals, including, in welfare organizations (Dunn et al., 2019), at laboratories (Newsome et al., 2019), grief management as a result of ending the life of an animal (Littlewood et al., 2020), as well as among veterinary professionals (Monaghan et al., 2020). According to veterinary nurse Thompson-Hughes (2019, p. 266), professionals of animal health are continually exposed to stressful situations in which they cannot always act in the "best standard of care to every patient." Such limitations of the profession often spark psychological distress due to an accumulation of violent or traumatic experiences. As a result, the quality of care and professional commitment may be affected.

Caring professions are often engaged in trauma-related work. Vicarious traumatization (VT) is a psychological effect of trauma work on the emotional state and productivity of therapists exposed to traumatic stories (Pearlman & Saakvitne, 1995). The psychological consequences are often referred to as the "death of empathy." As a result, professionals change their perception of themselves, others, and the world as it also impacts their motivation, efficacy, and empathy (Baird & Kracen, 2006, p. 182). Thus, repeated exposure to animal suffering also carries a psychological cost on the ability to perform care.

Another psychological response to trauma-related work is secondary traumatic stress (STS). STS and VT are similar cognitive phenomena, but the former is specific to therapists with similar symptoms to people coping with post-traumatic stress disorder: "Professionals who listen to reports of trauma, horror, human cruelty and extreme loss can become overwhelmed and may begin to experience feelings of fear, pain and suffering similar to that of their clients" (Gentry, 2002, p. 41). STS has been identified for veterinary professionals and compassion fatigue (CP) is a common term explaining the psychological struggle of those in the veterinary profession (Thompson-Hughes, 2019). CP is a burnout with symptoms of exhaustion, avoidance, and numbing in professional relationships due to the cumulative stress of experiencing violent and traumatic situations.

Regardless of psychological terminology, exposure to traumatic events may impact professionalism. Rauvola et al. (2019) identify a more complex cognitive response to trauma-related work. The empathy-based stress (EBS) encompasses VT, STS, and CP and is defined as "a stressor-strain-based process of trauma at work, wherein exposure to secondary or indirect trauma, combined with empathic experience, results in empathy-based strain and additional outcomes" that can affect work, behaviors, and cognitions (Rauvola et al., 2019, p. 299). Although "secondhand trauma" (e.g., witnessing, hearing about trauma) and "empathic engagement" (i.e., a function of individual differences, emotional norms and expectations) are conditional on poor mental health, the authors identify contextual and individual factors (Rauvola et al., 2019, p. 298). As examples of contextual factors, the authors list emotional display norms and expectations, form and frequency of trauma exposure, and support. Individual factors refer to sociodemographic, empathy-relevant individual differences, personality, and coping strategies. These are the four components to EBS which are the condition to "adverse occupational health and wellbeing outcomes" (e.g., burnout, depression, anxiety) and "negative work affect, behaviours, and cognitions" (e.g., performance, turnover, satisfaction). In addition to the aforementioned structural arrangements and studies on psychological consequences of trauma work, EBS might influence the ability of administrative veterinarians to make empathic decisions while stamping animal use and abuse as they usually have worked at the front-line of the profession.

FROM INDIRECT PARTICIPATION THROUGH THE V-STAMP TO CRIMES AGAINST THE ANIMALS

Contemporary societies have normalized the exploitation of many species based on speciesist discrimination that further benefits capitalistic interests for profits on behalf of the grievous commodification of animals' bodies. The normalization of animal abuses for trivial human desires is legitimized by the authority of veterinary expertise. Administrative veterinarians who work for government or laboratories have in their grasp the power to participate in policies and guidelines to deal with how animals' bodies should be exploited for economic profit—likewise, how to maximize use and abuse. Such veterinary stamps are important contributions to the exploitation of animals on farms and in laboratories that should not be overlooked. Accordingly, a V-Stamp on animal consumption and experimentation is undeniably an indirect participation in violence and should be considered criminal acts.

In Canada, some violent crimes committed by and on human beings are referred to as homicide, rape, and sexual assault. Every year, the raping and the premeditated killing of billions of female, and male, terrestrial and aquatic animals occurs in legitimized food and science institutions. Under speciesism, such mass exploitation and permissible killing of animals validates these violent crimes. Violent crimes committed against animals during a lifetime of exploitation as well as their murder have not been recognized as malefactions yet. If we look at the definition of crimes against humanity, we can easily make the connection between what is socially a wrongdoing between humans but acceptable and common practices towards animals as policies and guidelines are established for economic purposes. Indeed, crimes against humanity refer to

> murder, extermination, enslavement, deportation, imprisonment, torture, sexual violence, persecution and any other inhumane act of omission committed against civilians, in a widespread or systematic manner, whether or not the country is in a state of war, and regardless if the act is in violation of the territorial law in force at the time
> (Government of Canada, 2016).

We should concur that the definition of crimes against humanity can similarly be applied to animals, as they are the silenced and hidden victims of the cruelest of human activities. Open and undercover animal rights and liberation activists have played key roles in providing glimpses into farms (factory or familial), and laboratories (Best & Nocella II, 2004). Most practices on animals' bodies are so gruesome that many people do not want to watch the footage or will attempt to deny the authenticity of the images. As stated by Beirne (2018, p. 23), "human actions that cause the deaths of animals" (e.g., factory farming and testing industries) constitute *theriocide*, which is the equivalent of human-to-human killing. As crimes against humans are political misdeeds, indirect and direct participation in theriocide should be considered a crime and must be acknowledged and deemed as major infringements on animals' bodies.

As administrative veterinarians participate in the regulation of the exploitation of animals' bodies, they are accomplices to a violent speciesist system that has commodified animals. Their expertise carries the authority to justify "welfare" policies. Such administrative approval is legitimized due to a structural arrangement that also justifies the exploitation of animals' bodies as a speciesist stock of knowledge presents animals as inferior to humans and refers to them as mechanical bodies without capacity for reflectivity or feelings. This ideological arrangement has transformed animals into lively commodities without fundamental rights.

Although a dimension of the veterinary profession is speciesist, there is still a socio-psychological dimension to the role of administrative veterinarians in regulating crimes against animals for profit. As moral disengagement is a condition for maintaining animal exploitation, veterinarians need to understand their role within the mainstream stock of knowledge because this role is essential to vile industries in establishing economic rules to legitimize lawful exploitation of animals. Thus, administrative veterinarians are key players in fallacious welfare policies and violent crimes against animals. In addition, the veterinary profession engages in trauma-related work. Injured, sick, sometimes mutilated and soon-to-be euthanized or killed animals are quotidian of the care-providing profession. Experiencing continuous animal suffering on a regular basis has psychological and professional consequences. Normally, administrative veterinarians have done the front-line caring work. But the stressful situations in which they work might have a dramatic impact on their empathic judgment. Participation in animal welfare policies to accommodate animal profiteers at the expense of the animals themselves might also be the result of detached reflexivity from an atrophy of empathy in terms of care for animals.

In the final analysis, the V-Stamp is essential to the exploitation of animals but should be considered an indirect crime against animals; policies and guidelines provide lawful support to the abhorrent use of animals' bodies. Humans consider themselves superior to animals, but that is an imaginary construct without any basis in objective reality. Human superiority is a key element to the harmful and exploitative but legal interference on animals' bodies, and is a criminal exploitation and obfuscation of crimes in farms, slaughterhouses and high-security laboratories, it plays a decisive role in maintaining an economic status quo. It is important to realize that animals are not lesser beings than humans. Human superiority is an advantageous social construct for humans, rather than an objective reality. Namely, it is through animal welfare policies and guidelines which contain a speciesiest and unempathetic rhetoric that allows for criminal interferences on anonymized animals' bodies. The latter represent the mass victims of systemic oppression in which no one takes the responsibility for such large-scale crimes against animals. Regulation of abuse is also a crime, albeit indirect.

CONCLUSION

Animal exploitation subsists in speciesist cultures where everyone participates indirectly in harms towards animals, especially in a capitalist society. Yet, those who adopt an ethical vegan lifestyle contribute less to animal exploita-tion. Veterinarians who are involved in animal welfare policies in/directly take part in maintaining animals as commodities as their expertise "stamps" the regulation of abusive and cruel interferences on their bodies. Thus, a "V-Stamp" has cultural and economic dimensions of speciesism and capitalism, respectively. Such an arrangement not only normalizes animal exploitation but uses the veterinarian profession to maximize profits based on dubious animal welfare policies and guidelines. Investigating the veterinary profession and animal welfarism has pointed to a discussion of violent crimes against animals. It has been argued here that administrative veterinarians participate in structural violence towards the animals. Their legitimate expertise is essen-tial to crimes against animals, crimes that must be recognized and terminated. They contribute by establishing animal welfare documents for exploitative institutions. Though indirect, as they usually do not directly interfere with animals' bodies, this contribution is still a participatory contribution to the use and abuse of animals. Is the participation in structural mass violence more or less perverse than being the one who is the immediate abuser? Given the end result of continued exploitation and suffering, does it matter? Regardless, a lack of empathy is a key dimension of animal exploitation, be this through administratively stamped documents or more directly by a farm or laboratory employee.

The controversial and political discussion engaged in this essay also leads to a reflection on the concept of welfare—and most of the time the rejection of suf-fering. Although the absence of indirect involvement in animal exploitation, even to a lesser degree, is now structurally impossible, one should be critical of welfare policies and welfare reforms as they maintain a speciest and capitalist status quo rather than abolishing it as CAS seeks to accomplish. Furthermore, many are grateful to animal rights and liberation activists who investigate by risking their own freedom to expose animal abuses on farms and in laboratories, which are workplaces prone to animal welfare issues. With repressive "ag-gag" laws rising in Canada, only investigators can take the reality of animal exploitation outside of the walls of these criminal institutions to break free from any kind of domination and fulfill animal liberation.

ACKNOWLEDGMENT

I would like to thank every veterinarian who is committed to animal health and well-being. Although the profession is emotionally challenging, all of you still care and protect your silenced patients. I am also thankful to Dr. José López for editing and commenting on this essay.

REFERENCES

Agnew, R. (1998). The causes of animal abuse: A social-psychological analysis. *Theoretical Criminology*, *2*(2), 177–209.

Baird, D. K., & Kracen, A. C. (2006). Vicarious traumatization and secondary traumatic stress: A research synthesis. *Counselling Psychology Quarterly*, *19*(2), 181–188.

Bateson, P. (2011). Ethical debates about animal suffering and the use of animals in research. *Journal of Consciousness Studies*, *18*(9–10), 186–208.

Beirne, P. (2018). *Murdering animals: Writing on theriocide, homicide and nonspeciesist criminology.* Palgrave Macmillan.

Best, S., & Nocella II, A. J. (Eds.). (2004). *Terrorists or freedom fighters? Reflections on the liberation of animals.* Lantern Books.

Buttlar, B., & Walther, E. (2019). Dealing with the meat paradox: Threat leads to moral disengagement from meat consumption. *Appetite*, *137*, 73–80.

Canadian Animal Health Institute. (2020, June). *About us.* https://www.cahi-icsa.ca/about-us

Canadian Council on Animal Care. (2020, June). *Three Rs and ethics.* https://www.ccac.ca/en/three-rs-and-ethics/the-three-rs.html

Canadian Veterinary Medical Association. (2018, June). *A Career in veterinary medicine.* https://www.canadianveterinarians.net/documents/a-career-in-veterinary-medicine-handout-2018

de Waal, F. B. (2011). What is an animal emotion? *Annals of the New York Academy of Sciences*, *1224*(1), 191–206.

DuBois, J. M., Chibnall, J. T., & Gibbs, J. (2016). Compliance disengagement in research: Development and validation of a new measure. *Science and Engineering Ethics*, *22*(4), 965–988.

Dunn, J., Best, C., Pearl, D. L., & Jones-Bitton, A. (2019). Mental health of employees at a canadian animal welfare organization. *Society & Animals*, *1*(aop), 1–37.

Gentry, J. E. (2002). Compassion fatigue: A crucible of transformation. *Journal of Trauma Practice*, *1*(3–4), 37–61.

Government of Canada. (2014, June). *Provincial and territorial legislation concerning farm animal welfare.* https://www.inspection.gc.ca/animal-health/humane-transport/provincial-and-territorial-legislation/eng/1358482954113/1358483058784

Government of Canada. (2016, June). *War Crimes Program.* https://www.justice.gc.ca/eng/cj-jp/wc-cdg/prog.html#scope

Graça, J., Calheiros, M. M., & Oliveira, A. (2016). Situating moral disengagement: Motivated reasoning in meat consumption and substitution. *Personality and Individual Differences*, *90*, 353–364.

Haraway, D. J. (2007). *When species meet.* University of Minnesota Press.

Jasper, J. M. (1997). *The art of moral protest: Culture, biography, and creativity in social movements.* University of Chicago Press.

Littlewood, K. E., Beausoleil, N. J., Stafford, K. J., Stephens, C., Collins, T., Fawcett, A., Hazel, S., Lloyd, J. K. F., Mallia, C., Richards, L., Wedler, N. K., & Zito, S. (2020). How management of grief associated with ending the life of an animal is taught to Australasian veterinary students. *Australian Veterinary Journal*, *98*(8), 356–363.

Marx, K. (2011 [1867]). *Capital: A critique of political economy. Volume 1.* Dover Publications.

Mitchell, L. (2011). Moral disengagement and support for nonhuman animal farming. *Society & Animals*, *19*(1), 38–58.

Monaghan, H., Rohlf, V., Scotney, R., & Bennett, P. (2020). Compassion fatigue in people who care for animals: An investigation of risk and protective factors. *Traumatology*.

Newsome, J. T., Clemmons, E. A., Fitzhugh, D. C., Gluckman, T. L., Creamer-Hente, M. A., Tambrallo, L. J., & Wilder-Kofie, T. (2019). Compassion fatigue, euthanasia stress, and their management in laboratory animal research. *Journal of the American Association for Laboratory Animal Science, 58*(3), 289–292.

Nocella II, A. J., & George, A. E. (Eds.). (2019). *Intersectionality of critical animal studies: A historical collection*. Peter Lang Inc.

Nocella II, A. J., Salter, C., & Bentley, J. K. C. (Eds.). (2015). *Animals and wars: Confronting the military-animal industrial complex*. Lexington Books.

Nocella II, A. J., Sorenson, J., Socha, K., & Matsuoka, A. (Eds.). (2014). *Defining critical animal studies: An intersectional social justice approach for liberation*. Peter Lang Inc.

Nocella II, A. J., White, R. J., Cudworth, E. (Eds.). (2015). *Anarchism and animal liberation: Essays on complementary elements of total liberation*. McFarland.

Pearlman, L. A., & Saakvitne, K. W. (1995). *Trauma and the therapist: Countertransference and vicarious traumatization in psychotherapy with incest survivors*. W. W. Norton & Company.

Perret, J. L. (2020). *Mental health of veterinarians in Canada: Prevalence of outcomes, associations with veterinarian characteristics, and impacts on client perceptions of care* [Doctoral dissertation, University of Guelph]. http://hdl.handle.net/10214/17937

Rauvola, R., Vega, D., & Lavigne, K. (2019). Compassion fatigue, secondary traumatic stress, and vicarious traumatization: A qualitative review and research agenda. *Occupational Health Science, 3*(3), 297–336.

Ryder, R. D. (2000). *Animal revolution: Changing attitudes towards speciesism*. Bloomsbury Academic.

Schütz, A. (Author) & Wagner, H. R. (Ed.). (1999). *Alfred Schutz on phenomenology and social relations*. University of Chicago Press.

Thompson-Hughes, J. (2019). Burnout and compassion fatigue within veterinary nursing: A literature review. *Veterinary Nursing Journal, 34*(10), 266–268.

Vollum, S., Longmire, D., & Buffington-Vollum, J. (2004). Moral disengagement and attitudes about violence toward animals. *Society & Animals, 12*(3), 209–235.

Wu, C.-H. (2020). The influence of mindfulness and moral disengagement on the psychological health and willingness to work of civil servants experiencing compassion fatigue. *Current Psychology* (New Brunswick, Nj), 1.

CHAPTER SIX

The Phaeton Conflict in Turkey: The Case of Animal Domination in Istanbul Adalar

DENIZ HOSBAY BAYRAKTAR

Today, nonhuman animals are exploited in many ways. For example, the meat industry is one of the largest industries in the world. In this industry, which focuses on minimum cost and maximum profit, nonhuman animals are loaded with growth hormones to provide rapid growth, and nonhuman animals are kept in extremely narrow spaces to reduce inventory costs. This causes inflammation in nonhuman animals due to immobilization, and this inflammation is attempted to be prevented through high amounts of antibiotics. This is something people often neglect in the content of the packaged meat on their plates. Besides the bodies of nonhuman animals, there are various areas where their labor is exploited. For example, in some countries, nonhuman animals have started to be exploited as workers. One of the most recent examples of worker nonhuman animals is monkeys used to harvest coconuts. While a human collects about 80 coconuts a day, a monkey collects 1,000 pieces a day. Some of the teeth of the worker monkeys are pulled out for easier training and the monkeys are housed in cages (Tayland'in Isci Koleleri, 2020). The way people exploit nonhuman animals continues even in wars. For example, in World War I, glow-worms were used to read battle reports at night. Sometimes nonhuman animals were even used as living weapons in wars (Nocella et al., 2015).

One form of exploitation of nonhuman animal labor takes place through the phaetons (a primitive transport vehicle mostly horse-drawn, also known as carriages). In Turkey, as well as other places throughout the world, phaetons have been used for many years. The most intensely used place was Adalar (district of Istanbul). Adalar, also known as Prince Islands, is a group of nine islands of various sizes. There are settlements in Sedef Island, Heybeliada, Burgazada, Kinaliada. There are no permanent and regular settlements in Sivriada (Hayirsizada), Yassiada, Kasik Island and Rabbit Island. Although there are other alternatives, today nonhuman animals continue to be used in transportation in Adalar. Five hundred horses die annually due to phaetons in Adalar; this exploitation and death continues despite the protests of many animal rights activists and some inhabitants of Adalar. With the change of the mayor of Istanbul in June 2019, a workshop about the phaetons was organized in September 2019 and the parties came together but no result could be reached. After this meeting, it was explained that the horses were infected with glander disease with the additional effect of unhealthy conditions and 105 horses were killed because of it. The other horses in the region were quarantined and use of the phaeton was largely canceled during the three-month period with the help of radical activists' protests.

This chapter will express how the exploitation, domination and oppression of power is realized through phaetons. It will also explain the systematic exploitation of horses, the attacks of phaeton owners, the struggles of radical animal rights groups who opposed the hierarchical politics that allowed the exploitation of the horses used for the phaetons, inhabitants of the Adalar, and the state's response to these actions.

The Adalar case reveals that hierarchical, speciesist, neoliberal ideologies lead to the exploitation of the horses. The scholar-activist field of Critical Animal Studies (CAS) explicitly opposes such circumstances on the grounds of "advanc[ing] a holistic understanding of the commonality of oppressions … viewed as parts of a larger, interlocking, global system of domination" (Nocella et al., 2014, p. xxvii). Further, CAS "advance[s] an anti-capitalist and radical anti-hierarchical politics to dismantle all structures of exploitation, domination, oppression, torture, killing, and power in favor of decentralizing and democratizing society at all levels and on a global basis" (Nocella et al., 2014, p. xxvii). Thus, viewed from a CAS perspective, the existence of phaetons is significantly problematic for many reasons.

Around 1,500 horses and 272 carriages had been used for phaetons at Adalar, and around 500 horses used to die in this domination due to poor working conditions every year. This situation has been the subject of debate for many years. There are four different parties involved with the phaeton debate in Adalar. These are:

- Phaeton Owners
- Inhabitants of the Adalar

- The State (Istanbul Metropolitan Municipality-IMM)
- Animal Rights Activists

Phaeton owners maximized their profits and reduced their costs by operating their horses with minimum food and water. Despite some exceptions of humans taking good care of their horses, the phaeton system in Adalar was systematic exploitation. Phaeton owners tried to legitimate themselves on the grounds that they followed their father's profession; they stated that the phaeton was their only means of living and a symbol of Adalar.

Across the citizens of Adalar, there are two views. Some inhabitants agreed that horses are systematically tormented and support the abolition of phaetons. Some of the people who have been living on the island for a long time want to use phaetons in their daily life. They think it is a symbol of the rhythm and spirit of Adalar.

Regulating authority of transportation on the Adalar largely belongs to the Istanbul Metropolitan Municipality (IMM). The phaeton issue has been a problem ignored by the IMM for years. Although activists had protested, the usage of phaetons had been going on for a long time. The previous mayors of the Adalar did not want to lose votes and did not dare to abolish the phaetons due to the existing number of phaetons and their families in Adalar. But with the change of mayors, came a new attitude of the state towards the phaetons.

NGOs have struggled against the use of phaetons in the Adalar for years (against both the state and phaeton owners). The main theme of this struggle has been to explain to the public that using phaetons means dominating the horses in a system of exploitation. New horses were brought to the place of the destroyed ones, as in the slave market. While a horse can live for an average of 25 years, the life of horses running on a phaeton is only two years. Activists claimed that horses lost their lives unnaturally; their corpses converted into money (sent to slaughterhouses immediately) and they were rapidly replaced by other horses brought by boats. The main aim of activists was not fewer carriages or better living conditions for horses, but the complete removal of the phaeton system. The actions and wishes of these organizations in the context of total liberation are in line with the mission and goals of CAS (Nocella & George, 2019; Nocella et al., 2019). Their request was to give horses the right to live freely (Basin Aciklamasi, 2015). In their actions and press releases, they stated that the systematic exploitation led to the deaths of thousands of horses.

Animal rights struggles in Adalar in particular and in the world in general can be examined within the scope of new social movements. The term social movement was first used by Saint Simon in the early eighteenth century. Simon used this term to characterize social protest movements, first seen in France and then in other countries. Originally the term was used as a feature of the new political forces that opposed the status quo, and then its meaning expanded in time and now it most commonly includes wider political groups and organizations (Yanik & Ozturk, 2014). The term social movement reflects the organized effort of a significant number of people to change (or resist the change of) one or more of the main characteristics of the society (Scott & Marshall, 1999). Brecher and Costello (1999) argue that seeing other people share similar experiences, perceptions and feelings opens the way for a new set of possibilities. This group formation process builds new solidarity and this solidarity helps bolster social movements.

In the 1960s, social movements began to change. The demands of new social movements have evolved; they started to demand more democratic and egalitarian life conditions rather than economic reforms (Yanik & Ozturk, 2014). The new social movements began to focus on the issues related to the life, such as the body, health and sexual identity, the neighborhood, the city and the physical environment; cultural, ethnic and national heritage and physical life conditions and the continuation of humanity and also natural life, environment and anthropocentrism issues (Offe, 2009).

Technological development affected the characteristic features of the social movements. Technological transformation has changed the network of relations. At this point, the internet provides an excellent post-social environment. Individuals interact through keyboards, computer screens, websites, email, chat rooms, massive multiplayer games, and so on. In some cases, internet relationships include also face-to-face interactions (Ritzer, 1996). Virtual platforms today are indispensable for democratic actions and movements. Today one of the most important things is the techno-policy of global resistance. The internet stands out in this area. There are now broad areas of political struggle and places where new voices can be heard. The use of these technologies by radical activists appears to be highly democratic and is generally free of commodity characteristics. These technologies open up new areas for sustaining campaigns against governments and global corporations (Ritzer, 2009).The internet helps animal activists organize and raise awareness and support for causes very far away from one's location (Best & Nocella, 2004; Nocella et al., 2014).

With the spread of new social movements, many organizations have been established in the field of animal rights struggle. The number of NGOs established in this context is quite high. According to the current data of the ministry of internal affairs, the number of official associations in the category of Animal Protection is 2418 in Turkey (Derneklerin Faaliyet Alanlarina,2020). In addition, there are many active animal protection platforms and initiatives that are unofficial, organized only through social media. The term of "animal protectionism" may be a suitable and relevant term to explain that a large number of people are concerned with animal abuse and rights issues. Generally these people come from various ideological backgrounds (Taylor, 2004). Munro uses the term "animal movement" as an umbrella term for the more specific terms such as animal protection movement, animal welfare movement, animal liberation movement and animal rights movement in his studies (Munro, 2002, 2005, 2012). The term "animal protectionist" involves anyone who supports the animal movement on a continuum from animal welfare through to animal rights.

Nelkinand Jasper (1992) classifies American animal protectionists using three categories: "welfarists," "pragmatists," and "fundamentalists." Francione (1996) puts animal protectionists into a general categorization as "animal welfarist" and "animal rightist." Animal welfarists strive to regulate the domination of animals, while animal rightists endeavor to abolish animal exploitation (Francione, 1996; Munro, 2005). Through his dissertation and book, Munro (2002, 2005) considered animal protection as a social movement and classified protectionists as animal welfarist, animal rightist or animal liberationist. In 2012, Munro stated that an additional classification is needed for extensively defending animal defenders and included this group in his classification as "Radical Animal Liberation Movement" (Munro, 2012). One of the prominent radical animal liberation groups in the world is Animal Liberation Front (ALF). Animals that are used/killed for human benefit are rescued by members of the ALF by actions such as raiding fur manufacturing factories, destroying hunters' weapons and ammunition depots, and emancipating the nonhuman animals in laboratories (Best & Nocella, 2004; Nocella et al., 2019).Carrying out radical actions around the world, ALF members in Turkey have carried out actions such as damage to the pet-shops and hunting clubs, and organizing marches against slaughterhouses. While these classifications provide a nice overview of how animal protection—broadly conceived—is generally thought about, for CAS, nothing short of intersectional total liberation is an acceptable goal. Theory is derived from experience in radical activism that revolves around this desired outcome (Nocella et al., 2014).

Although the struggle for animal rights is taken up in the context of new social movements, it has a remarkable history in Turkey. The first animal protection association (named Istanbul Himaye-I HayvanatCemiyeti—Istanbul Society for the Protection of Animals) in Turkey was established in 1912, after the Hayirsizada Massacre. Around 80,000 dogs were left to Hayirsiz Ada on the grounds that they might have rabies and all the dogs died from starvation. Following the establishment of the Republic, the organization named Turkish Society for the Protection of Animals was established as a continuation of the Istanbul Society for the Protection of Animals and started to operate in 1924 (Gurler et al., 2011). Throughout the Republic, many organizations were established in this field. The most important development for nonhuman animals in Turkey is "Animal Protection Law Number 5199" issued in 2004 with the efforts of the animal protectors and organizations. This law was criticized by animal rights organizations for not being fully comprehensive, and many negative incidents took place in the country. The phaeton problem is one of them.

THE DEVELOPMENTS OF THE PHAETON CONFLICT IN ADALAR

Phaetons have been in Turkey for many years in many cities to satisfy the nostalgic feelings of people. Horses exposed to exhaust smoke and forced to work on hot asphalt were employed in various provinces of Turkey as a result of an anthropocentric view of nonhuman animals as means to human ends. With the increasing number of animal protectors and better organizing via social media, the domination of nonhuman animals via the phaeton started to be opposed. Activists have come together on the internet since 2014 under the name of "Do not Use Phaeton Horses are Dying Platform" (Faytona Binme Atlar Oluyor Platformu). Another platform doing serious work in this field is the "The Horses of Adalar Platform" (Adalarin Atlari Platformu). These platforms, which were established by a group of people who frequently met with the Mayor of Istanbul Metropolitan Municipality Ekrem Imamoglu and aimed to follow closely the processes related to the phaetons, took an active role throughout the process, both informing the public and organizing. Like many animal protectionist platforms that oppose the use of phaetons, these platforms have focused their attention on Adalar. The approximately 1,500 horses and nearly 300 phaeton cars in Adalar constitutes serious animal exploitation. The working conditions of the horses used as the main means of transport were horrible (Nazi Kampi Gibiydi, 2019):

> The phaeton owner sews up the horse's wound, pours powdered sugar on it and paints it with the same color as the horse's shoe polish ... Most colts are thrown off the cliff or given to live dogs because it is expensive to grow up ... Blood accumulates on the wrists of horses due to getting rushed too much. The phaeton owners pull it with an injector. Although horse entry to Adalar and exit is prohibited, many horses are brought to the island by boats every season. And then, while those horses are pulled to the island, some of them die by getting their legs caught by the boat's engine.

In Adalar, horses were running on asphalt fstreets. In order to satisfy the tourists, the horses worked for hours without any break, sometimes until 3 am. Do not Use Phaeton Horses are Dying Platform stated that the phaeton system was a complete exploitation system and the phaeton system should have been abolished and eliminated completely. Every year around 400 horses die due to extremely bad working conditions (Faytona Binme Atlar, 2017).

Even though the phaeton struggle on the Adalar started many years ago, the first concrete step by the municipality was taken with the left party CHP (Cumhuriyet Halk Partisi-Republican People's Party) candidate winning the IMM in the 2019 Local Elections. Since the transportation in Adalar was under the control of the Municipality of Istanbul, the mayors of Adalar took a passive position on the phaeton conflict. The previous mayors of IMM, who could have solved this problem, did not put it on their agenda. Generally, the administration of Istanbul has been under the control of right-wing parties. In the elections held in March 2019, there were strong candidates of two different parties as Istanbul Metropolitan Municipality Mayor candidates: Ekrem Imamoglu-CHP (left) and Binali Yildirim-AKP (right). Although Ekrem Imamoglu won in the elections held on March 31, 2019, it was decided to vote again with various claims and in the second election held on June 23, 2019, Imamoglu became the mayor of Istanbul.

During the candidacy, Imamoglu made a promise to solve the persecution of the phaetons and signed the document on which the demands of the animal protectors were written. Turkish animal rights defenders and animal protectors trusted and voted for Imamoglu. Since the carriages are under the control of IMM, Adalar Mayor Erdem Gul did not take any initiative like the former mayors. The captive horses were mistreated by the phaeton owners with only three to four hours of breaks per day, often were seriously wounded, and frequently became sick. Eighty-one horses with glander disease were slaughtered and buried in a deep hole. After this massacre, phaetons were banned in the district for three months.

Animal liberation advocates set up a tent in front of the IMM building on December 19, 2019 to hold a "Life Watch" in order to account for the increasing deaths (it was later revealed that 24 more horses died). As animal rights activists who do not adopt welfare policies, they wanted the phaetons to be removed completely, to provide electric phaetons/vehicles, and to relocate horses to a living area where they will live freely and be rehabilitated (Atli Faytonlar Kalkti, 2020). Activists holding the "Life Watch" in front of the IMM building met with Imamoglu and after learning that 5% of phaetons would remain for symbolic purposes; they declared that they would continue to hold the "Life Watch" until all the phaetons got removed and this watch continued for days (Tebrikler Baskan Cagin, 2019).

About the death of horses, 347 animal rights, and environment and nature associations published a jointly signed press release (c'da oldurulen 81 at icin 347 olusumdan ortak basin bildirisi, 2019), and animal rights activists in the "Life Watch" read the press statement in front of the Istanbul Metropolitan Municipality. The activists drew attention to the ambiguity of the method followed for the detection of the disease and the non-transparency of the process, and also stated the fact that the glander disease had turned into a public health problem. These are the demands of animal protectors (Adalarda Oldurulen 81 At, 2019):

- Taking the necessary measures for the health of all living beings in Adalar at the highest level and expanding the scope of quarantine if necessary,
- Conducting an investigation against all authorized institutions and responsible persons who do not provide the horses with the necessary health conditions,
- Sharing with the public the tests and laboratory results applied to horses with diseases, as well as the method of killing used and to be used on diseased horses,
- Putting ecological transportation alternatives into effect in Adalar as soon as possible,
- Abolishing the exploitation of horses and providing opportunity to spend their remaining lives freely.

One of the activists stated that at least 30 veterinarians are needed for 1,800 horses and said, "Istanbul Metropolitan Municipality is a big municipality in terms of its possibilities. It is not a municipality that cannot allocate funds for horses" (Adalar'da En Az, 2019).

After all these developments, the struggle that lasted for years finally yielded results on January 31, 2020. Imamoglu announced the decision that all phaetons would be removed in Adalar. The activists thanked Imamoglu for this decision (Ekrem Imamoglu Sozunu, 2020). After this decision, animal rights activists, who were on a "Life Watch" action, ended their protests on the 41st day. IMM decided to purchase 277 registered phaetons for 300 thousand TL and six horses for 4,000 liras per phaeton. It has been decided that the transportation would be carried out by electric vehicles to be operated by IMM and the horses would be left to the natural habitats of the Ministry of Agriculture and Forestry under veterinary control. Thus, Imamoglu reversed his own decision to keep 35 symbolic phaetons for tourism purposes. Animal rights activists stated that after this process, they will follow the survival of nearly 1,300 horses that had been exploited and worked under the persecution of phaetons for years, and their transportation (Atli Faytonlar Kalkti, 2020; Adalar'da FaytonlarinYerine, 2020). Later, there were a few people who wanted to own the horses free of charge, but this situation drew a big reaction among the animal protectors. The activists claimed that these horses would be slaughtered and demanded that the municipality prevent this (Adaların Atlari Adalar'da, 2020). Meanwhile, some horse owners agreed not to use their horses with the phaeton, but did not want to sell their horses, and continued to feed their horses like pets (Adalar'da Ruam Karantinasi, 2020). Within the framework of the horse liberation plan, firstly it was decided to take the horses purchased by the Municipality to the tents set up in the quarantine stable in Buyukada, and to transfer these horses from the island. In the stable in Buyukada, during the quarantine process, the horses that were not detected with glander disease were taken out by the groomers at certain intervals and these horses were exercised (Adalar'da Atlari Satin, 2020).

Upon the purchase of the phaeton in Adalar and the horses driven on the phaeton by the IMM, a division resulted among phaeton owners. Some phaeton owners, who were opposed to selling their phaetons to IMM, organized a sit-in protest in Buyukada. The phaeton owners who organized the protest stated that they would not accept the money given to them by IMM and they wanted to continue operating their phaetons (IBB'nin Fayton Kararina, 2020). Stating that they had been promised a new job by IMM before, the phaeton owners claimed that this promise was not kept. The phaeton owners stated that they would continue the protest until the promises given to them were kept (Faytoncuların Ekmek Isyani, 2020).

Due to the late arrival of electric vehicles, which are planned to be used instead of carriages, transportation problems were experienced in Adalar at the beginning of summer. Although it was prohibited, vehicles called "tuk-tuk" were used for a while (Faytonlarin Yasaklandigi Adalar'da, 2020).

After the horses were bought by IMM and brought to the stables in Adalar, animal protectors made a new statement and claimed that the conditions of the horses were not good, they remained inactive in the stables, and many of them died. In addition, animal protectors calculated that 396 horses were missing, based on previous data. Animal protectors demanded that the horses not be given to butchers outside Adalar and that they spend their lives in the forests of Adalar (Adaların Atlari Adalar'da, 2020). After the banning of phaetons in Adalar, IMM started to adopt the horses, and departments such as Veterinary Faculty, Equine and Horse Trainer Departments of various universities started to adopt the horses of Adalar (IBB, Adalar'daki Fayton, 2020). In June 2020, usage of electric vehicles has started instead of phaetons in Adalar (Faytonlarin Yerine Bunlar, 2020). However, some inhabitants also did not like the new electric vehicles and stated that these vehicles did not look nice and nostalgic for Adalar. They argued that the new vehicles looked like bulky buses (Adalar'da Fayton Yerine, 2020).

It is necessary to make a point here. When the above-mentioned news in the newspapers of Cumhuriyet and Yenisafak are examined, two different approaches can easily be seen. While the leftist newspaper Cumhuriyet, which supports Imamoglu, reflects the positive developments in Adalar, the rightist newspaper Yenisafak which is against Imamoglu, carried criticisms in its columns. Istanbul is also very important politically due to being the most populous city in Turkey. Istanbul was ruled by right-wing parties (except between 1989 and 1994) between 1984 and 2019. In Turkish politics there is a widespread belief: *The party that gets control of Istanbul can easily get ruling authority of the whole country in the future.* The current President also served as the Mayor of Istanbul in the past. The ruling party holding the central government did not want to lose the city that has such a political importance and the elections in March 2019 were renewed, but Imamoglu also won the second election. Therefore, while the leftist press tends to support Imamoglu, the right-wing press criticizes him and tries to prevent his influence from spreading across the country. It is thought that Imamoglu will be a rival to the current president Erdogan in the 2023 Presidential Elections (Muhalefet Partilerinde Cumhurbaskani, 2020).

After the electric vehicles came to Adalar, the Adalar District Governorship vetoed these vehicles on the grounds that they did not comply with the Traffic Law, but this problem was resolved after the negotiations between the Governorship and the Municipality (Ekrem Imamoglu, Adalar'daki, 2020). After the phaetons were removed, a group of demonstrators also organized a protest to bring the phaetons back, but this demand was met with a great negative reaction from the majority (Atlari Boyle Gormek, 2020). The Horses of Adalar Platform made a statement on June 22, 2020 and stated that the horses were imprisoned in the stables and the horses should be liberated. In addition, the platform stated that they did not want motor vehicles in Adalar and argued that people would be transported to every corner of Adalar together with motor vehicles, which may cause forest fires. The leader of HAYKURDER (Hayvanlari Koruma Kurtarma ve Yasatma Dernegi—Animal Protection, Rescue and Survival Association) stated that electric phaetons should be used and they would not accept horse-drawn phaetons under any circumstances. The famous artist, the Founding President of the HACIKO Association (Hayvanlari Caresizlik ve Ilgisizlikten Koruma Dernegi—Association for the Protection of Animals from Desperation and Indifference), stated that the torture in Adalar has ended with the decision of the IMM and claimed that those who say "Let the phaeton come back" are not the real inhabitants of Adalar (Soybas, 2020). While these developments were taking place, the new situation was also criticized from the left.

Animal protectors, who argue that the process of adopting horses should be more transparent, organized a campaign called "Let the Horses Live in Adalar" on the internet and collected more than 21,000 signatures. The group handed over these signatures to IMM and stated that horse deaths in Adalar continue and the condition of the horses should be improved as soon as possible. Animal protectors also shared the good news that the horses were taken out of the stables and they won the opportunity to move (Adaların Atları Adalar'da, 2020). In July 2020, a leftist newspaper supporting Imamoglu also published a report stating that the general condition of the horses owned by Istanbul University was very good. In the news, it was stated that the horses owned by the Horse Trainer Department were free and happy and recovered from depression (Adalar'dan Ozgurluge Kosan, 2020).

The struggle, which continued for many years, was resolved in 2020 as requested by activists and the use of phaetons in Adalar is currently prohibited. Animal rights NGOs criticized the disruptions in the process after the prohibition of phaetons and demanded the correction of these disruptions. As a result of these pressures the disruptions have been largely corrected and the horses are now in a better position than before.

CONCLUSION

Although Turkey's capital is Ankara, Istanbul attracts many local and foreign tourists. One of the popular places for these tourists is Adalar, which is very close to Istanbul. The phaeton had been used as a means of transportation in Adalar for many years, and due to the ongoing horse deaths and systematic domination, it attracted many people, especially animal protectors and animal rights advocates.

For days, animal rights organizations protested the decision that phaetons should remain for symbolic reasons. When the decision was taken to abolish the phaetons completely, they thanked the mayor; afterwards, they criticized the issues such as insufficient health services and poor conditions of the stables, lack of transparency regarding adopting horses. For this reason, while the statements of animal rights advocates, who stand in a more politically objective position, constitute the main context of the study, the news of right-wing and left-wing newspapers on phaetons was also added.

To summarize, the domination of horses through the use of phaetons that lasted for many years has been resolved by passing through the following stages: Thanks to the organization of animal rights groups, public pressure has been created and the leftist party candidate has prevailed in local governments. This leftist mayor, which values living beings relatively more, has taken steps to solve the problem and met with all actors. Thus, the problem of phaetons that caused the most horse deaths in Turkey ended. The problem, which could not be solved by the rightist parties, was solved together with the left party in one year. In this struggle that has been going on for years, animal rights activists have organized and have held many demonstrations especially in the last year. In the solution of the phaeton issue, it has been observed that the determined struggles of animal rights platforms and activists were very effective rather than the approach of the leader.

REFERENCES

Adalar'da atlari satin alma islemi basladi [Buying horses begins in Adalar]. (2020, February 14). https://www.sozcu.com.tr/hayatim/yasam-haberleri/adalarda-atlari-satin-alma-islemi-basladi/amp/

Adalar'da fayton yerine elektrikli arac kullanimi begenilmedi [The use of electric vehicle instead of phaeton in Adalar was not liked].(2020, June 14) https://www.yenisafak.com/gundem/adalarda-fayton-yerine-elektrikli-arac-kullanimi-begenilmedi-3544825

Adalar'da en az 30 veterinere ihtiyac var[Need at least 30 veterinarians in Adalar]. (2019, December 30). https://m.haberturk.com/buyukada-da-en-az-30-veterinere-ihtiyac-var-2554304-amp

Adalar'da faytonlarin yerine gelen elektrikli araclari IETT isletecek [The municipality will operate the electric vehicles that replace the phaetonsin Adalar]. (2020, February 13). https://www.haberler.com/adalar-faytonlarin-yerine-gelen-elektrikli-12916796-haberi/

Adalar'dan ozgurluge kosan atlar! Eski hallerinden eser kalmadi [Horses to freedom from Adalar! There is no trace of their old forms]. (2020, July 20). https://www.gercekgundem.com/istanbul/198589/adalardan-ozgurluge-kosan-atlar-eski-hallerinden-eser-kalmadi

Adalar'da Ruam karantinasi bitti! Ahirlarin yikimina baslandi [Ruam quarantine finished in Adalar! The destruction of the stables has begun]. (2020, March 25). https://www.hurriyet.com.tr/gundem/adalarda-ruam-karantinasi-bitti-ahirlarin-yikimina-baslandi-41477809

Adalar'in atlari Adalar'da yasasin! Kasaplara, serum ureticilerine gitmesin! [Let the horses of Adalar live in Adalar! Don't let horses go to butchers, serum manufacturers!]. (2020, March 30). https://www.change.org/p/adalar%C4%B1n-atlar%C4%B1-adalar-da-ya%C5%9Fas%C4%B1n-tc-istanbul-adalarkaymakam-yavuzerkt-tonguccoban-ekrem-imamoglu-Atları şöyle görmeyi protesto ettiler: Vicdan nerede?]. erdemmgul/u/26179549?cs_tk=Ah9ltaxhumQsHSt-Dh14AAXicyyvNyQEABF8BvPHcyMclmhd8c371i13e3pM%3D&utm_campaign=b0a590d2b0744410a791f1ce42cb63cc&utm_content=initial_v0_4_0&utm_medium=email&utm_source=petition_update&utm_term=cs

Atlari soyle gormek icin sokaga cikip protesto yaptilar: Vicdan bunun neresinde? [They protested to see the horses like this: Where is the conscience?]. (2020, June 19). https://www.yenicaggazetesi.com.tr/atlari-boyle-gormek-icin-sokaga-cikip-protesto-yaptilar-vicdan-bunun-neresinde-285086h.htm

Atli faytonlar kalkti, eylem sona erdi! [Phaetons banned, the protest ended!]. (2020, January 28). https://www.sozcu.com.tr/2020/gundem/atli-faytonlar-kalkti-eylem-sona-erdi-5593216/amp/

Basin aciklamasi– 31 Mayis 2015 [Press release—31 May 2015]. (2015, June 01). https://faytonabinmeatlaroluyor.wordpress.com/2015/06/01/basin-aciklamasi-31-mayis-2015/

Best, S., &Nocella, II, J. A. (2004). *Terrorists or freedom fighters: Reflections on the liberation of animals*. Lantern Books.

Brecher, J., & Costello, T. (1999). *Global village or global pillage: Economic reconstruction from the bottom up*. South End Press.

c'da oldurulen 81 at icin 347 olusumdan ortak basin bildirisi [Joint press statement from 347 associations for 81 horses killed in Adalar]. (2019, December 19). https://gaiadergi.com/adalarda-oldurulen-81-at-icin-347-olusumdan-ortak-basin-bildirisi/

Derneklerin faaliyet alanlarina gore dagilimi [Distribution of associations by their fields of activity]. (2020, June). https://www.siviltoplum.gov.tr/derneklerin-faaliyet-alanlarina-gore-dagilimi

Ekrem Imamoglu, Adalar'daki fayton kararinin ardindan konustu [Ekrem Imamoglu speaks after the decision of the phaeton in Adalar]. (2020, June 19). https://www.cumhuriyet.com.tr/haber/ekrem-imamoglu-adalardaki-fayton-kararinin-ardindan-konustu-1746092

Ekrem Imamoglu sozunu tut, Istanbul Adalar'da fayton devrini kapat [Ekrem Imamoglu keep your words, finish the phaeton period in Istanbul Adalar]. (2020, January 31). https://www.change.org/p/ekrem-imamo%C4%9Flu-s%C3%B6z%C3%BCn% C3%BC-tut-istanbul-adalar-da-fayton-devrini-kapat-ekrem-imamoglu-faytonlary asaklans%C4%B1n-faytonsuzistanbul/u/25680939?cs_tk=AtSUv1v-MRSKAMAdOF4AAXicyyvNyQEABF8BvLPIVBidWw1nAa2ivX-_TyI%3D&utm_campaign= cb775a0840024b1685dfb05b28acf35e&utm_content=initial_v0_2_0&utm_medium=email&utm_source=petition_update&utm_term=cs&fbclid=IwAR0DA6fYXmpdTpPELdfkNCl3U-PAAVEiRMcR_Z0M4xIvuD4_K1nhvIVooz0

Faytona binme atlar oluyor, konuk: Elif Erturk [Do not use phaeton horses are dying, guest: Elif Erturk]. (2017, August 11). https://www.youtube.com/watch?fbclid=IwAR11- xmcBLZhfi_wyJMKA6dMQfgb9awnS8Ef54r7heSI2IiPd3VTFkizVMg&v=PZQYG8e0D54&feature=share&app=desktop

Faytoncularin ekmek isyani! IBB ve Adalar Belediyesi sozunu tutmadi [The riot of the phaeton owners! IMM and Adalar municipality did not keep their words]. (2020, February, 20). https://www.sabah.com.tr/video/haber/faytoncularin-ekmek-isyani-ibb-ve-adalar-belediyesi-sozunu-tutmadi-video

Faytonlarin yasaklandigi Adalar'da bu kez de baska bir ulasim krizi cikti [Another transport crisis occurred this time in Adalar where phaetons were banned]. (2020, June 06). https://www.sondakika.com/haber/haber-adalar-da-ulasim-sorunu-elektrikli-faytonlar-icin-13297237/

Faytonlarin yerine bunlar kullanilacak [These will be used instead of the phaetons]. (2020, June 13). https://www.posta.com.tr/faytonlarin-yerine-bunlar-kullanilacak-2261136

Francione, G. L. (1996). Animal rights: An incremental approach. In R. Garner (Ed.), *Animal rights the changing debate* (pp. 42–60). Macmillan Press. https://doi.org/10.1007/978-1-349-25176-6

Gurler, A. M., Melikoglu, B., & Osmanagaoglu, S. (2011). A historical evaluation of animal protection efforts of non-governmental organizations in Turkey. *Kafkas University Veterinary Faculty Journal, 17*(6), 901–908. https://doi.org/10.9775/kvfd.2011.4665

IBB, Adalar'daki fayton esnafindan aldigi 177 ati sahiplendirmeye basladi [IMM started to adopt 177 horses acquired from phaeton owners of Adalar]. (2020, June, 08). https://www.cumhuriyet.com.tr/haber/ibb-adalardaki-fayton-esnafindan-aldigi-177-ati-sahiplendirmeye-basladi-1743792

IBB'nin fayton kararina oturma eylemi [Sitting protest against the IMM's phaeton decision]. (2020, February, 15). https://www.ensonhaber.com/amp/ic-haber/ibbnin-fayton-kararina-oturma-eylemi

Muhalefet partilerinde cumhurbaskani adaylari ve ittifaklarin hangi senaryolar konusuluyor? [Which scenarios for presidential candidates and alliances are discussed in opposition parties?]. (2020, September, 11). https://www.bbc.com/turkce/haberler-turkiye-54112783

Munro, L. (2002). *Beasts abstract not: A sociology of animal protection* [Unpublished Doctoral Dissertation]. Monash University.

Munro, L. (2005). *Confronting cruelty: Moral orthodoxy and the challenge of the animal rights movement*. Brill Academic Pub.

Munro, L. (2012). The animal rights movement in theory and practice: A review of the sociological literature. *Sociology Compass, 6*(2), 166–181. https://doi.org/10.1111/j.1751-9020.2011.00440.x

Nazi kampi gibiydi ... Atlara eziyeti bir de benden dinleyin [It was like a Nazi camp ... Listen the torment of the horses from me]. (2019, December, 29). https://www.hurriyet.com.tr/gundem/nazi-kampi-gibiydi-atlara-eziyeti-bir-de-benden-dinleyin-41408075

Nelkin, D., & Jasper, J. (1992). *Controversy: Politics of technical decisions.* Sage.

Nocella, II, J. A., & George, E. A. (Eds.). (2019). *Intersectionality of critical animal studies: A historical collection.* Peter Lang.

Nocella, II, J. A., Drew, C., George, E. A., Ketenci, S., Lupinacci, J., Purdy, I., & Schatz, L. J. (Eds.). (2019). *Education for total liberation: Critical animal pedagogy and teaching against speciesism.* Peter Lang.

Nocella, II, J., Salter, C., & Kentley, C. K. J. (Eds.). (2015). *Animals and war: Confronting the military-anima industrial complex.* Lexington Books.

Nocella, II, J. A., Sorenson, J., Socha, K., & Matsuoka, A. (Eds.). (2014). *Defining critical animal studies: An intersectional social justice approach for liberation.* Peter Lang.

Offe, C. (2009). *Yeni sosyal hareketler: Kurumsal politikanin sinirlarini zorlanmasi* (K. Cayir, Trans.) [New social movements: Challenging the boundaries of institutional politics]. Kaknus Yayin. (Original work published 1985).

Ritzer, G. (1996). *Postmodern social theory.* McGraw-Hill College.

Ritzer, G. (2009).*Globalization: A basic text.* Wiley-Blackwell.

Scott, J., &Marshall, G. (1999). *Sosyoloji sozlugu* (O. Akinhay & D.Komurcu, Trans) [A dictionary of sociology]. Bilim ve Sanat Yayinevi.(Original work published 1994). https://doi.org/10.1093/acref/9780199533008.001.0001

Soybas, Fulya. (2020, June22). https://www.hurriyet.com.tr/yazarlar/fulya-soybas/adalarda-fayton-donemi-bitti-sorun-bitmedi-41547130

Tayland'in isci koleleri: Maymunlar [Thailand's labor slaves: Monkeys]. (2020, July 05). https://www.ntv.com.tr/galeri/dunya/taylandin-isci-koleleri-maymunlar,azi4r7lMrkuPsL-Rnc5w5pA

Taylor, N. (2004). In it for the nonhuman animals: Animal welfare, moral certainty, and disagreements, *Society & Animals, 12*(4), 317–339. https://doi.org/10.1163/1568530043068047

Tebrikler Baskan! Cagin %5 gerisinde kaldiniz [Congratulations, Mayor! You are 5% behind the age]. (2019, December 21). https://gaiadergi.com/tebrikler-baskan-cagin-5-gerisinde-kaldiniz/

Yanik, C., Ozturk, M. (2014). Toplumsal hareketlerin donusumu uzerine bir degerlendirme [An assessment on the transformation on social movements]. *Mukaddime, 5*(1), 45–63. https://dergipark.org.tr/tr/pub/mukaddime/issue/19677/210139

A Comparison of the Local Governments in Terms of Approaches to Stray Animals in Turkey

DENIZ HOSBAY BAYRAKTAR AND OZGUR BAYRAKTAR

When the history of Turkey is examined, it is apparent that the attitudes of the local administrations towards stray animals differ according to the ideology of the mayor. Stray animals have been perceived as a problem for municipalities in Turkey since the early days of the republic. Even before the republic—during the Ottoman Empire—the number of stray animals were very high. In order to reduce this number, the Ottoman administration carried out various massacres. The largest massacre for stray animals is the Hayirsizada Massacre in 1910. Eighty thousand dogs were taken to the island and left to die. Although the people who tried to protect the nonhuman animals and established foundations for them opposed this situation, they could not prevent it. Further massacres were carried out by poisoning stray animals. Local administrations carried out some of the biggest massacres in the past. In Turkey, some mayors tried to find a solution without killing stray animals, while some mayors and governors gave rifles to the people and asked them to shoot the stray dogs and paid them for each corpse (Pinguet, 2009; Gundogdu, 2018; Fortuny, 2014).

This study investigates the approaches towards stray animals made by the state, with special attention to local governments. After examining the struggle for animal rights in the world and in Turkey historically, the approaches of the municipalities in Turkey towards stray animals are discussed comparatively. In this study, it is concluded that animals are more exposed to oppression, torture and killing during the period of right-wing market-oriented neoliberal parties.

While the approach taken is that of a Critical Animal Studies (CAS) perspective, it is particularly compatible with the 5th principle of (CAS) which "Rejects apolitical, conservative, and liberal positions in order to advance an anti-capitalist and, more generally, a radical anti-hierarchical politics. This orientation seeks to dismantle all structures of exploitation, domination, oppression, torture, killing, and power in favor of decentralizing and democratizing society at all levels and on a global basis" (Nocella et al., 2014, pp. xxvii). In order to achieve this, the ways in which local governments legitimize the killing of stray animals in Turkish history will be discussed.

In this context, practices of right-wing municipalities and left-wing municipalities are compared. The difference in the approach of the municipalities under the rule of two different mentalities to stray animals in Turkey and the issues on which these municipalities differ are examined. This study is also an interdisciplinary study as it is related to local governments, the approach of the state to animals and animal liberation, further aligning it with CAS because CAS encourages interdisciplinary studies and collaboration (Nocella et al., 2014).

ANIMAL RIGHTS MOVEMENT IN THE WORLD AND TURKEY

Developments and trends in animal welfare and animal rights around the world have affected Turkey. Peter Singer is a pioneer of animal welfare approaches, and he has a utilitarian perspective in his famous book *Animal Liberation* (Singer, 1975). According to this view, there is a principle of equal consideration and this principle should be applied to all animals that are capable of feeling. Singer follows a moral approach that allows animals to be used for the benefit of people. In this respect, animals can continue to be exploited when the interests of the animal and the interests of the human are conflicting and the human interest is deemed more important. According to the utilitarian view, if exploitation is to exist, this exploitation should be carried out with the least pain possible, and animals should not be subjected to unnecessary suffering. Singer has been duly criticized. Gary Steiner (2005) emphasized in his book, *Anthropocentrism and Its Discontents: The Moral Status of Animals in the History of Western Philosophy*, that there is a problem with calculating the interests taken by the utilitarian approach according to pleasure and suffering because it is people who make these calculations and thus it is likely they will make decisions anthropocentrically.

Similarly, David DeGrazia (2006) considers the idea that animals have moral rights insufficient. Moral rights emphasize that animals should not be subjected to unnecessary suffering, and that they should be treated morally. Although animals have rights in this sense, according to this view, their interests should not be violated without good reason.

Tom Regan (2003), on the other hand, argues that animals have moral rights and that the exploitation of animals should be eliminated altogether rather than preventing the exploitation of animals in poor conditions. According to Regan, all animals that are the "subject of a life" should be able to benefit from these rights. Gary Francione argues that the consideration of animals as property means that they will continue to be seen as objects with no significant interests (Francione, 2008). Going beyond these theoretical developments, CAS has gained importance. CAS aims to critically examine the relationship between the human and nonhuman animals by rejecting speciesism, sexism, racism, ableism, statism, classism, militarism and other hierarchical ideologies (Nocella et al., 2014, 2019; Nocella & George, 2019). It aims to do this through radical grassroots activism and supporting other total liberation efforts, such as the Animal Liberation Front (Best & Nocella, 2004).

While these discussions and developments were taking place in the world, various developments took place in Turkey; the animal rights struggle in Turkey has progressed since the 1980s. Before then, the animal rights struggle was not very strong. However, if a starting point is mentioned, the year 1910 is seen as a milestone.

When examining the perspective of animals in the history of Turkey, it is seen that the developments in Istanbul are quite determinant. Before Republic, during the Ottoman period, the modernist members of Ittihat ve Terakki Cemiyeti (Union and Progress Association) saw stray dogs as an obstacle to modernization and got into the cause in 1910 (Tarih, 2016). Despite the resistance of the people, 80,000 dogs were gathered from the streets and left on the island of Hayirsizada to die from hunger and thirst (Fortuny, 2014). Animal activists affected by this massacre tried to establish an association but could not successfully organize. A Spanish company that came to Istanbul in 1912 wanted to organize bullfights but activists opposed it. In this event, when animal protectors acted together and got results, it was decided to establish the first animal protector association of Turkey, the Istanbul Himaye-i Hayvanat Cemiyeti (Istanbul Animal Protection Association) (Gundogdu, 2018). One of the two main aims of the society was the prevention of cruelty and injustice towards animals. The second aim was to work towards increasing the love of animals in society. The society wanted to increase the punishment to be given to those who mistreated animals, and to make new laws and regulations about animals. When World War I broke out in 1914, the activities of the association ceased (Pinquet, 2009). With the directives of Ataturk, it continued its activities as "Turkey Animal Protection Association" shortly after the founding of the Republic and started its activities on March 6, 1924. The association was a social club in the early days, trying to organize tea parties and express a love of animals, but it was not very visible (Melikoglu, 2009). The association assumed the role of "humane" culling of animals and continued this activity until the 1990s. Thousands of animals were killed in the gas chamber in the association's hospital by so-called "humane" methods (Pinquet, 2009; Topcuoglu, 2010). In the 1920s and 1930s, the Istanbul Municipality started poisoning dogs again on the pretext of lack of vehicles. The association donated dog grapples and a car to the municipality.

In addition to the society, a new association was established. But, founded in 1934 under the leadership of the Dutch ambassador's wife, the "Ankara Animal Protectors Association (Ankara Hayvan Severler Cemiyeti)" was soon closed. Then, on December 12, 1945, a new association called "Ankara Animal Compassion and Relief Society (Ankara Hayvanlari Sevme ve Yardim Cemiyeti)" was established and the number of animal protection organizations in Turkey increased to two.

The start of World War II in 1939 was the beginning of hard times for animals as well as for humans. Thousands of cats and dogs died from lack of food during WWII. Turkey Animal Protection Association, which continued its activities in the same line in the 1950s, received the status of a public benefit association on April 28, 1950, with the decision of the Council of Ministers. In 1955, another association was established, the Animal Protection Association (Hayvanlari Koruma Dernegi) in Ankara under the leadership of the President Celal Bayar (Yasar &Yerlikaya, 2004).

In the 1960s and 1970s, it is seen that the militant animal rights movement was on the rise in the USA and Europe, and also in Turkey. The revolutionary wave of 1968 also radicalized animal rights activists, putting the issue of animal rights on a completely different ground, rather than being considered just an "animal lover" issue. Various associations have also been established in Istanbul, such as the Association for the Protection of Natural Life (Yasar & Yerlikaya, 2004). One of the results of this struggle, which gained momentum in the 1970s, was the "Universal Declaration of Animal Rights," which was declared at the UNESCO house in Paris on October 15, 1978. The manifesto, which is based on the equality of all species, rejects the ordering of the universe in an anthropocentric hierarchy.

In addition to the increase in the number of associations in Turkey after 1980, there was a mental transformation. The most important reason for the change was the emergence of new environmental and animal rights organizations, including people who had been in political groups before September 12, and these organizations began to establish strong international links. The character of the struggle in Turkey has turned from loving of the animal to animal rights advocacy. In October 1991, the Animal Protectors Association started to prepare a draft law for the protection of animals (Sungurbey, 1992). Thanks to new formations and international connections, the first victory of the transformed struggle was about bears dancing on the street. In 1992, the World Animal Protection Foundation (WSPA) created a shelter for bears in Bursa, and since 1993 it was strictly forbidden to make bears dance in the streets (Tarih, 2016). Many associations were established such as the Foundation for the Protection of Natural Life in 1996, the Association of Those Who Love Nature and Animals, and the Association of Environment and Street Animals in 2003 (Yasar & Yerlikaya, 2004).

During this period, animal rights NGOs often struggled with municipalities that treated animals badly. In addition, they pressed the Parliament to change the existing animal rights law with activities such as protests and signature campaigns. In addition, NGOs organized various protests against animal-use companies during this period. "Animal Protection Law Number 5199" issued in 2004 was the result of efforts of the animal protectors and organizations. According to the Law no.5199, the animals have to be sterilized and then left where they are taken. NGOs forced the municipalities to implement this law completely. Animals that are unable to live outside are able to live in shelters (Sozer, 2007). After the animal protection law was passed, various violations were experienced and enforcement was lacking due to legal gaps. Organized animal rights activists frequently formed public opinion through various means such as protests, press releases, sit-ins and signature campaigns, and tried to prevent such violations by putting pressure on the state and administrators, especially local governments.

APPROACHES OF LOCAL GOVERNMENTS TOWARDS STRAY ANIMALS IN TURKEY

Within the context of approaches by local governments to street animals, the most prominent examples of municipalities' approaches to stray animals as reflected in the media are analyzed. The media coverage of animal rights abuses in Turkey was seen only after 1980 because the abuse and killing of stray animals was quite commonly accepted before 1980. For years, even the Turkey Animal Protection Association was helping municipalities under the name of "humanitarian methods" in the culling of stray animals. In this section, first the practices of right-wing municipalities and then the approaches of left-wing municipalities are discussed since the 1980s.

RIGHT-WING CASES

After the September 12, 1982 coup, during the period of Abdullah Tirtil, who was appointed as the Mayor of Istanbul by the military government, a huge wave of cat and dog massacres started. President Tirtil announced that 26 teams start killing stray animals to fight rabies in July 1983 and asked for support from the public. Bedrettin Dalan from ANAP (Anavatan Partisi—Motherland Party), who was elected Mayor of Istanbul in 1984, made a statement saying, "I will bring men from Korea and feed them all of the stray dogs." Dalan did not bring men in from Korea, but did start a massive cat and dog hunt. In 1987, in Izmir, Mayor Burhan Ozfatura (from ANAP) and Governor Vecdi Gonul started a cat and dog culling campaign and asked support from the public. In July it was also revealed that Ekrem Barisik the mayor of Bursa (from ANAP) burned 1,747 cats and dogs in an oven. In April 1989, Tokat's new mayor, Ismet Saracoglu (from DYP, Dogruyol Partisi—True Path Party) closed the zoo and killed nearly 400 animals. It was revealed that Saracoglu sold camels, gazelles and the other animals whose meat was suitable for eating to butchers (Sungurbey, 1992).

In March of 2000, Denizli Baklan Mayor Ayhan Demirdover (from DYP) organized dog fights. Around 250 shepherd dogs were forced to fight in Denizli Baklan Stadium. The animals were blinded and their ears were severed, and more than 2,000 citizens, including mayor Demirdover, watched this brutal demonstration. Mayor Demirdover said: "We had an income of 1 billion 100 million lira from fights. Do not despise poor people's entertainment. Local people love dog fighting, we organized it too. There is nothing to be exaggerated" (Kopek Dovusturen Baskan, 2000; Belediyeden "Vahset" Hizmeti, 2000). On January 23, 2005, the person who was against Elazig Kovancilar Municipality (from Saadet Partisi (SP)—Felicity Party) team's striking street dogs was shot down by a rifle (Aksu & Korkut, 2017). It was claimed that the donkeys used in collecting the garbage were starved during the striking period of 420 workers in the Mardin Municipality (from SP) in March 2006. The head of the labor union of Mardin branch, stated that the donkeys' situation was very poor due to the municipality's lack of feed, and that some of them died (Aksu & Korkut, 2017).

In February 2011, the Erzurum Municipality (from AKP, Adalet ve Kalkinma Partisi-Justice and Development Party) and HAYTAP (Hayvan Haklari Federasyonu-Animal Rights Federation) started a cooperative project. In the project, words and messages addressing animal rights in terms of religion were exhibited on billboards (Aksu & Korkut, 2017). In December 2012, the municipality which poisoned stray dogs in Erzurum's Hinis district, made a statement that "we wanted to put them to sleep, but the drug dose was too high." The mayor of Hinis Municipality Enver Tacyildiz (from AKP) said: "There are many dogs on the streets. The people are constantly complaining. They ask us to 'Shoot the dogs, kill them.' We do not poison the animals; we just numb them. If the central government supports us, we can build a shelter, but we have no budget now" (Hinis'ta Kopek Katliami, 2012).

Since 2015, another current debate in the animal rights field is about the Istanbul Kisirkaya shelters. The animal rights protectors assert that the animals who died in the shelters of the State died due to bad conditions. NGOs filed a lawsuit to block the opening of a high capacity Kisirkaya Shelter because they thought that this shelter would have worse conditions than the existing small shelters. NGOs' struggle on this issue still continues (Aksu & Korkut, 2017). On January 2, 2018 at around 9 pm, two cleaning staff working in Agri Kagizman Municipality shot two dogs. Deputy Mayor of Kagizman Halit Erguven (from AKP) said, "There were two dogs but these were not killed as claimed. They fainted and delivered to the shelter. They are alive." According to the information obtained, it was learned that there was no animal shelter in the region (Belediye Suc Ustu, 2018). In July 2018, a citizen who applied to the police in the Gulsehir district of Nevsehir, complained that the municipal teams shot and killed three dogs in the playground. After the images were posted on social media and some websites, a big reaction grew. Gulsehir Mayor Vahdi Arisoy (from MHP, Milliyetci Hareket Partisi—Nationalist Movement Party) claimed that the news was completely wrong and was biased, and said: "I called our employees who were involved in the incident and they told me that they only sprayed plants and didn't kill dogs. However, a few dead dogs were also found in that park. We have started an investigation against those responsible" (Belediye Ekibinin Kopekleri, 2018). In December 2019, Bafra Mayor Hamit Kilic (from AKP) made observations at the Stray Animals Rehabilitation and Care Center with a group of animal protectors. Kilic said: "It is our motto to love the creature because of the creator. We believe that every living thing has a right to life and we must respect it. The stray animals are entrusted to us by Allah" (Baskan Kilic Hayvanlar, 2019). Konya's Meram District Municipality took care of stray animals that had a hard time in cold weather. In a statement made by the Veterinary Affairs Directorate of Meram Municipality, it was reported that the teams distributed about 60 tons of food for dogs and five tons for cats in 2019 to the nutrition centers (Meram Belediyesi'nden Sokaktaki, 2019).

In February 2020, an animal protector complained about the Kocaeli Golcuk Municipality (from AKP), claiming that one of the stray dogs she fed was killed by animal gathering teams with an excessive amount of drug needles, one of her dogs was missing, and an abandoned building was destroyed while the puppies were inside it (Kocaeli'deki o Belediye, 2020). Also in February 2020, a citizen in Kocaeli wrote a petition to the Darica Municipality (from AKP) regarding the nonprocedural taking of the dog he was feeding on the street. Darica Municipality replied "Stray dogs cause visual pollution" to the petition given by the citizen. The citizen also claimed: "Dogs are left within the boundaries of the district. Dogs trying to return to the town perish on the way. They leave the dogs elsewhere and do not feed them there" (AKP'li Belediyeden Tepki, 2020). More bad news in February 2020 came from Siirt. It was learned that stray dogs were collected in a vehicle belonging to the municipality of Siirt Sirvan (from AKP). Eyewitnesses stated that municipal staff used a mechanism that was placed on the throats of animals to collect the stray dogs and dragged the stray dogs on the ground with this device. Despite the witnesses, it is unknown where the collected dogs were taken (AKP'li Siirt Sirvan, 2020).

LEFT-WING CASES

The first case was seen in June 2017 where it was claimed that some dogs in Yalova Municipality (from CHP, Cumhuriyet Halk Partisi—Republican People's Party) animal shelter were killed. The municipality has been fined regarding the issue (CHP'li Belediyeye Barinakta, 2017). In December, an animal protector revealed that the staff of Zonguldak Municipality (from CHP) gave drugs to ten dogs and then buried them alive (CHP'li Belediyeden Kopek, 2017). There was good news in March 2018 from Mugla Mentese Municipality (from CHP). Ten cat houses were placed in various parks by municipal teams. It was stated that the teams would check the cat houses from time to time to meet the food and water needs of the cats (Sokak Kedileri Yeni, 2018; Mugla Belediyesi Kedi, 2018). In January 2019, Izmir Metropolitan Municipality (CHP) announced the first aid center, where Stray Animals Emergency Response Team worked, had restored about 11,000 stray animals since 2014. Also, an animal ambulance of the center works at certain times of the day. In addition, the municipality offers a cemetery for those whose pets have died (Sahipsiz Hayvanlari Koruyor, 2019). Istanbul had been ruled by right-wing parties for twenty five years (1994–2019). During this period, stray animals and their rights were mostly ignored. With the win of the leftist candidate Imamoglu in 2019, positive developments in the field of animal rights occurred. When he was a candidate, he had promised to protect rights of all animals in Istanbul by signing the text of the Animal Rights Legislative Monitoring Delegation in March 2019. Also, he promised that greater emphasis would be placed on animal rights, that children starting from the primary school level would be made conscious of this issue, and adoption of stray animals would be promoted. He stated that modern rehabilitation centers would be established by providing a natural environment for stray animals (Istanbul Buyuksehir Belediyesi, 2019). In April 2019, after winning the election, Turkey's first communist mayor (from TKP, Turkiye Komunist Partisi—Turkey Communist Party) has made a call as follows: "Flower-gift will not be accepted to our municipality. The IBAN number below belongs to the stray animal care, treatment and rehabilitation center of our municipality. You can make your donations to this account..." (Macoglu, 2019).

Another development in April 2019 was seen at Izmir Menderes Municipality (from CHP) cooperated with HAYTAP and posted on billboards: "A cup of water, a cup of food" and "Help our friends!" One thousand food and water containers were made by the municipality and distributed to the shopkeepers. Also,

Menderes Municipality announced that it made 400 sterilizations in three months of 2019 (Izmir/Menderes Belediyesi, 2019). In June 2019, Ankara Metropolitan Municipality (from CHP) declared that the veterinary teams treated 9,695 stray animals in the past year. Municipal teams regularly leave food for street animals at certain locations in the city. In addition, the Metropolitan Municipality Temporary Nursing Home and Rehabilitation Centers serve for stray animals 24/7 with ten animal ambulances (Sahipsiz Hayvanlar Buyuksehir, 2019). In September 2019, with the decision taken by the Istanbul Avcilar municipality, fireworks were banned at Avcilar on the grounds that "they cause noise pollution, frighten migratory birds, and adversely affect human and environmental health." Avcilar Mayor Turan Hancerli (from CHP) said: "Our city has 357 kinds of birds every year; we have adopted the principle of respecting the right to life of every living thing" (Avcilar Belediyesi Havai, 2019).

According to the January 2020 statement of Antalya Metropolitan Municipality (CHP) Animal Health and Breeding Branch Directorate intervened in 9,000 notifications received in 2019 with a fully-fledged animal ambulance within the rehabilitation center. In the center, 969 cat and dog sterilizations, along with 96 orthopedics and fracture operations were performed. As well, 3176 rabies vaccines, 10,745 internal and external parasite vaccines, and 3,273 mixed vaccines were made, in addition to 209 stray animal adoptions (Buyuksehir'den Sokak Hayvanlarina, 2020). In April 2020, Izmir Buca Municipality announced that it treated 4,253 stray animals; sterilized 2,110; and vaccinated internal and external parasites and rabies on 2,500 animals. Also, it was stated that there was also a disabled cat care house with a capacity of 100 animals in the Stray Animals Rehabilitation Center (Sokak Hayvanlari Rehabilitasyon, 2020).

When compared, it is seen that there are various good and bad examples in right-wing and left-wing municipalities. However, when the examples reflected in the media are examined, it can be said that leftist municipalities are relatively more positive in their approach to stray animals. It is noteworthy that the left-wing cases are generally after the 2010s. The most important reason for this is that local governments in Turkey have been under the control of right-wing parties for many years. The low number of leftist municipalities led to less news coverage about stray animals. For this reason, it is natural that there are differences between the examples of right and left parties reflected in the media.

CONCLUSION

When the examples of coverage of stray animals as reflected in the media are examined, it is seen that municipalities headed by the left party have a more moderate approach to stray animals compared to right-wing municipalities. It is seen that right-wing municipalities frequently appear in the media promoting the abuse or killing of stray animals due to staff-related problems. In general, it has been determined that leftist municipalities provide more budget and opportunities for stray animals. It is also observed that leftist municipalities frequently cooperate with animal protection organizations. Although there are exceptions, it can be said that leftist municipalities observe the principle of respecting the right to life in protecting animals, and right-wing municipalities are said to treat animals as entrusted by God. While right-wing municipalities distribute food to animals, especially in winter, left-wing municipalities provide improved health and shelter services in addition to food distribution.

From the CAS point of view, it can be said that leftist municipalities are closer to the logic of the CAS in terms of respecting the right to life of animals, avoiding killing them, and not maintaining the existing domination order (Nocella et al., 2014). In addition, the cooperation of some left-wing municipalities with animal rights activists and NGOs brings them closer to the CAS logic. But there are more steps to take to get closer to CAS. For example, leftist municipalities may ban hunting altogether at the provincial borders, prohibit the sale of nonhuman animals instead of controlling the pet shop conditions. They can also take decisions to close the shops that sell fur at the provincial borders. And also, the employees who abuse animals in local governments should be fired.

In this comparison, in addition to the ideology, the following points should also be taken into account: As the struggle and organization for animal rights develops in Turkey, the value given to animals has increased. Therefore, the approaches of local governments, which are examined chronologically, are actually affected by the pressure of animal rights organizations and the public opinion. As a result, leftist municipalities that came to power in recent years are also reflected in the media with good examples. In summary, when a comparison is made in general, it can be said that leftwing municipalities in Turkey are in a relatively better position in approaching stray animals than right-wing municipalities.

REFERENCES

AKP'li Siirt Sirvan Belediyesi'nden sokak kopeklerine iskence! [Siirt Sirvan Municipality from AKP tortured stray dogs!]. (2020, February, 29). https://www.gazeteyolculuk.net/akpli—siirt—sirvan—belediyesinden—sokak—kopeklerine—iskence

AKP'li belediyeden tepki ceken cevap: Kopekler goruntu kirliligi [Answer of the municipality from AKP: Dogs create visual pollution]. (2020, February, 09). https://www.yenicaggazetesi.com.tr/akpli—belediyeden—tepki—ceken—cevap—kopekler—goruntu—kirliligi—267509h.htm

Aksu, C., & Korkut, R. (Eds.). (2017). *Ekoloji almanagi:2005—2016* [Ecology almanac: 2005—2016]. Yeni İnsan Yayinevi.

Avcilar Belediyesi havai fisegi yasakladi [Avcilar Municipality banned fireworks]. (2019, September, 07). https://www.birgun.net/haber/avcilar—belediyesi—havai—fisegi—yasakladi—267626

Baskan Kilic "Hayvanlar Bize Allah'in Emaneti" [Bafra Mayor Kilic: The stray animals are entrusted to us by Allah]. (2019, December, 21). http://www.bafra.bel.tr/Sayfa/5dfe8f79f-dcac1103cfeb92e/BASKAN—KILIC—"HAYVANLAR—BIZE—ALLAH—IN—EMANETI

Belediye ekibinin kopekleri oldurdugu iddiasiyla sikayetci oldu [The allegation that the municipal team killed the dogs]. (2018, July, 18). https://www.hurriyet.com.tr/belediye—ekibi nin—kopekleri—oldurdugu—iddiasiyl—40901007#:~:text=Zafer%20BARIŞ%2FNEVŞE HİR%2C%20(DHA,öldürdüğünü%20iddia%20ederek%2C%20şikayetçi%20oldu.&text= Grup%20bölgeye%20gittiğinde%2C%20bu%20kez%20de%20ölü%202%20köpek%20 gördü.

Belediye sucustu yakalandi! Kopekleri katlettiler [The municipality was caught! They killed dogs]. (2018, January, 04). https://www.sozcu.com.tr/hayatim/yasam—haberleri/belediye—suc—ustu—yakalandi—kopekleri—katlettiler/

Belediyeden "vahset" hizmeti ["Violence" service from the municipality]. (2000, March, 21). https://www.milliyet.com.tr/pembenar/belediyeden—vahset—hizmeti—5327099

Best, S., & Nocella, II., J. A. (2004). *Terrorists or freedom fighters: Reflections on the liberation of animals*. Lantern Books.

Buyuksehir'den sokak hayvanlarina yardim [Helping stray animals from the metropolitan municipality]. (2020, January, 06). https://www.cnnturk.com/yerel—haberler/antalya/buyukse-hirden—sokak—hayvanlarina—yardim—1470039

CHP'li belediyeye barinakta katliam cezasi [Punishment for massacre in shelter of CHP municipality]. (2017, June, 21). https://www.sabah.com.tr/yasam/2017/06/21/chpli—belediyeye—barinakta—katliam—cezasi

CHP'li belediyeden kopek katliami [Massacre of dogs from CHP municipality]. (2017, December, 17). https://www.takvim.com.tr/guncel/2017/12/17/chpli—belediyeden—kopek—katliami

DeGrazia, D. (2006). *Hayvan hakları* (H. Gur, Trans.) [Animal rights]. Dost Kitabevi. (Original work published 2002).

Fortuny, K. (2014). Islam, westernization, and posthumanist place: The case of the Istanbul street dog. *Interdisciplinary Studies in Literature and Environment, 21*(2), 271–297. https://doi.org/10.1093/isle/isu049

Francione, G. L. (2008). *Hayvan haklarina giris: Cocugunuz mu kopeginiz mi?* (E. Gen & R. Akman, Trans.) [An Introduction to Animal Rights: Your Child or Your Dog?] Iletisim Yayinlari. (Original work published 2000).

Gundogdu, C. (2018). The state and the stray dogs in late Ottoman Istanbul: From unruly subjects to servile friends. *Middle Eastern Studies, 54*(4), 555–574. https://doi.org/10.1080/00263206.2018.1432482

Hinis'ta kopek katliami! [Dog massacre in Hinis]. (2012, December, 11). http://www.erzurumolay.com/hinista—kopek—katliami—3959h.htm

Istanbul Buyuksehir Belediyesi CHP Baskan adayi Ekrem Imamoglu soz Verdi [Istanbul Metropolitan Municipality CHP President Candidate Ekrem Imamoglu made a speech]. (2019, April, 1). http://www.haykonfed.org/2019/04/01/13493/

Izmir / Menderes Belediyesi & HAYTAP ortak farkindalik calismasi [Joint awareness work from Izmir / Menderes Municipality & Haytap]. (2019, April 30). https://www.haytap.org/tr/izmir—menderes—belediyesi—haytap—ortak—farkindalik—calismasi

Kocaeli'deki o belediye ile ilgili kopek katliami iddiasi! [Dog massacre allegation about the municipality in Kocaeli!]. (2020, February, 24). https://www.kocaelibarisgazetesi.com/guncel/kocaeli—deki—o—belediye—ile—ilgili—kopek—katliami—iddiasi—2—h122353.html

Kopek dovusturen Baskan: 1.1 milyar kazandik [Mayor organized dog fighting: We earned 1.1 billion]. (2000, March, 21). https://www.hurriyet.com.tr/gundem/kopek—dovusturen—baskan—1—1—milyar—kazandik—39141460

Macoglu, Fatih. (2019). https://twitter.com/fatihmacoglu/status/1114117866943598592

Melikoglu, B. (2009). Turkiye'de kurulan ilk hayvanlari koruma derneginin tarihsel gelisimi [The historical development of the first society for animal protection in Turkey] *Veteriner Hekimler Derneği Dergisi, 80*(1), 37–44.

Meram Belediyesi'nden sokaktaki hayvanlar icin 65 ton mama [65 tons of food for stray animals from Meram Municipality]. (2019, December, 25). https://ajanimo.com/meram—belediyesinden—sokaktaki—hayvanlar—icin—65—ton—mama/

Mugla Belediyesi kedi evleri [Cat houses of Mugla Municipality]. (2018, March, 07). https://www.haytap.org/tr/mula—belediyesi—kedi—evleri

Nocella, II, J. A., & George, E. A. (Eds.). (2019). *Intersectionality of critical animal studies: A historical collection.* Peter Lang.

Nocella, II, J. A., Drew, C., George, E. A., Ketenci, S., Lupinacci, J., Purdy, I., & Schatz, L. J. (Eds.). (2019). *Education for total liberation: Critical animal pedagogy and teaching against speciesism.* Peter Lang.

Nocella, II, J. A., Sorenson, J., Socha, K., & Matsuoka, A. (Eds). (2014). *Defining critical animal studies: An intersectional social justice approach for liberation.* Peter Lang.

Peter, S. (1975). *Animal liberation: A new ethics for our treatment of animals.* HarperCollins.

Pinguet, C. (2009). *İstanbul'un köpekleri* (S. Ozen, Trans.) [The Dogs of Istanbul] Yapi Kredi Yayinlari.(Original work published 2008).

Regan, T. (2003). *Animal rights, human wrongs: An introduction to moral philosophy.* Rowman & Littlefield Publishers.

Sahipsiz hayvanlari koruyor ve tedavi ediyoruz [We protect and treat stray animals]. (2019, January, 24). https://www.izmir.bel.tr/tr/Projeler/sahipsiz—hayvanlari—koruyor—ve—tedavi—ediyoruz/1459/4

Sahipsiz hayvanlar Buyuksehir korumasinda [Stray animals under the metropolitan municipality protection]. (2019, June, 13). https://ankara.bel.tr/haberler/sahipsiz—hayvanlar—buyuksehir—korumasinda

Sokak hayvanlari rehabilitasyon merkezi ve hayvan ambulansi [Stray animals rehabilitation center and animal ambulance] (2020, April, 29). http://www.buca.bel.tr/Hizmetlerimiz/19/sokak—hayvanlari—rehabilitasyon—merkezi—ve—hayvan—ambulansi/hizmetlerimiz.html

Sokak kedileri, yeni yuvalarina kavustu [Stray cats have begun staying in their new home]. (2018, March, 07). https://www.mentese.bel.tr/sokak—kedileri—yeni—yuvalarina—kavustu/

Sozer, M. (2007). *Hayvan haklari mevzuati* [Animal Rights Legislation]. Adalet Yayinevi.

Steiner, G. (2005). *Anthropocentrism and its discontents: The moral status of animals in the history of Western philosophy.* University of Pittsburgh Press. https://doi.org/10.2307/j.ctt6wrcwf

Sungurbey, I. (1992). *Hayvan haklari: Bir insanlık kitabi* [Animal Rights: A Humanity Book] Istanbul University Law Faculty.

Tarih, December 2016 Vol. 31.

Topcuoglu, U. S. (2010). *Istanbul ve sokak kopekleri* [Istanbul and stray dogs]. Sepya Yayinlari.Yasar, A., & Yerlikaya, H. (2004). Dunya'da ve Turkiye'de hayvan haklarinin tarihsel gelisimi [Historical development of animal rights in Turkey and in the World] *Vet Bil Dergi, 20*(4), 39–46.

Afterword

WILL BOISSEAU

As I write this Afterword, reflecting on the important and diverse chapters from these radical emerging voices in Critical Animal Studies, we are still experiencing the collective uncertainty and dread caused by coronavirus. In England, we are still officially in a national lockdown, with the government advising people to stay at home, leaving only where permitted by law. In the UK, as with other countries in which contributors to this collection live, the criminal and murderous mishandling of the crisis by an incompetent and callous ruling class has led to hundreds of thousands of unnecessary deaths. The kleptocracy led by Boris Johnson in the UK has used the crisis as an opportunity to redistribute wealth from the people to the billionaire class, this crony capitalism has seen millions of pounds of government money handed to associates of politicians for contracts that are never fulfilled. Whilst the pandemic raged, the Conservative government has used the opportunity to further their ultimate aim of stealthily privatizing our National Health Service to US health insurance giants. People in the UK, and elsewhere around the world, have come to realize that the old maxim, that States exist to protect their citizens, has turned out to be a lie. In Britain, the ruling class do not care if people live or die.

I read this book at a time of despair and pessimism, a time spent fearing for the health and safety of family, whilst many comrades and friends have lost love ones over the past twelve months. However, throughout the year 2020 we have also seen the seeds of hope, and the Students for Critical Animal Studies have helped sow these seeds. This book emerged during a time of global resistance: during the fight for Black Lives Matter globally, the rise of Black Trans Lives Matter, the upsurge of the Reclaim the Streets feminist movement, mass strikes and protests in India, the End SARS protests in Nigeria, global climate strikes, and a victory for social democracy in Bolivia. Since the pandemic began, anarchist-inspired mutual aid groups have blossomed around the world as people realize that government's will not protect them in times of crisis, and that all people have is each other. After audacious leftist campaigns in the last five years to obtain high political office with the Corbyn project in the UK and for Bernie Sanders in the USA, it is clear that the emerging post-covid protest wave will take activists back on the streets in a non-hierarchical and militant direction.

The collection you've just read is particularly inspiring because it emerged from Students for Critical Animal Studies, and brings together voices from the new wave of radical politics. This collection shows the diversity of approaches needed, and that these different tactics are beneficial and necessary as we confront the class enemy who thrive on the exploitation and destruction of humans, other animals and the planet. It's important to critically analyze developments in radical politics and nurture emerging voices because when one protest wave does not achieve its ultimate objective, we need to learn from that, adapt, dust ourselves off and go again. As this collection shows, a diversity of tactics is necessary: activists will continue to achieve victories through direct action, and leftists can bring about benefits for humans and animals through municipal governments, as Deniz Hosbay Bayraktar and Ozgur Bayraktar show was achieved for stray animals in Turkey.

It's important to listen to and learn from diverse struggles as we aim to create a global movement for social justice. It is also vital for white male scholars to recognize that that they are not qualified to speak about the experience of oppression at the intersection of race and gender. Clearly, theory and activism by those at the forefront of gender, racial and class oppression have been at the vanguard of grounding animal liberation and Critical Animal Studies as radical non-hierarchical praxis that has made animal liberation a radical social movement. The Institute for Critical Animal Studies (ICAS) is doing excellent work in creating a platform for new emerging voices, and in particular for marginalized voices in academia (including People of Color, people with disabilities, and LGBTQ+ scholars). ICAS bring scholar-activists together in a respectful, nurturing and emboldening way.

Amongst the pessimism caused by economic injustice, increasing extinction rates, zoonotic diseases and ecological disaster, readers of this book will find optimism in the fact that activists remain undefeated and that wherever there is injustice, there is also resistance.

CAS scholar-activists should be just as inspired by our previous fights for social justice, the ongoing battles against oppression and the emerging and future struggles. Such a perspective reminds us that there is no final victory and no final defeat, and each generation will have to fight battles for liberation. Activists inspired by Critical Animal Studies want to completely transform society, we want to live without hierarchy and oppression; we believe that capitalism has caused ecological disaster and we want to build just and sustainable communities that work for the majority, not just the privileged few. When we picture the world we want to live in, it is not a world where countless human and non-human animals are killed in brutal and demeaning conditions. We are unapologetic about our radical vision of a world without exploitation. CAS scholar-activists make no reformist demands to the bourgeois State, instead we want to dismantle all structures of oppression and hierarchy by building the three intersecting liberation movements for human, animal and Earth liberation. CAS scholar-activists believe that no one form of liberation is possible without the others – as they would still be rooted in oppressive societies which rely on the logic of domination and hierarchy.

No matter how hopeless or how far such a world appears, it is only by daring to dream of radically different futures that we will develop the movements that are strong enough to bring a better world into existence. This book is part of that struggle, and will inspire readers to continue to build coalitions for social justice. Although it may not be in our lifetimes, the day will come when we build communities in which peace and social justice for humans, animals and the Earth can thrive. The struggle carries on.

Contributors' Biographies

Deniz Hosbay Bayraktar is a research assistant in the Department of Management and Organization at Karamanoglu Mehmetbey University. She graduated from Business Administration at Dokuz Eylul University in 2008. In 2013, she completed her MA in Business Administration at Akdeniz University. Deniz also graduated from Anadolu University Associate Degree Veterinary Department in 2012. Now she is a doctorate student in the department of Management and Organization in Yildirim Beyazit University, preparing a thesis about Animal Rights Organizations in Turkey. Having been a vegetarian for 20 years, Deniz has been interested in protecting animals and treating stray animals since she knew herself. She lives with three disabled cats and two dogs.

Ozgur Bayraktar has been a research assistant in the Department of Political Science at Karamanoglu Mehmetbey University since 2011 and graduated from Public Administration at Dokuz Eylul University in 2011. In 2012, Ozgur started his MA in Political Science at Hacettepe University and received his MA degree in 2016 with his dissertation titled *Separation at Nationalist Movement: Nationalist Movement Party and Grand Unity Party*. Ozgur is a PhD student at Hacettepe University, Department of Political Science and currently writing a dissertation titled *Being the Other in Turkey: Staying out of the Nationalist Conservative Framework*. He lives with three disabled cats and two dogs.

Annie Bernatchez is a doctorate student in sociology. As a political sociologist in the fields of social movement and critical *studies*, her research interests focus on emotion, animal liberation, activism, and criminalization in Canada. She has started her fieldwork to investigate the everyday lives of Animal Liberation activists within the current social context of state repression that categorizes such forms of activism as terrorism. Annie will hold to an anti-speciest standpoint throughout her thesis to advocate against such categorization. She is the co-director for students at the Institute for Critical Animal Studies and advisor for Vegan Option Canada.

Will Boisseau, Ph.D., completed his doctorate at Loughborough University in 2015. His research focuses on the place of animal rights within the British left, particularly on the relationship between the anarchist/direct action and legislative wings of the movement. His work explores the class and gender issues influencing this relationship, the marginalization of animal rights in mainstream labor politics and a range of concepts including speciesism, total liberation, critical animal studies and intersectionality. Will is currently involved in trade union politics in the UK.

Allison Gray is a doctorate Candidate at the University of Windsor, studying across multiple perspectives involving food crime, green criminology, consumerism, vegan criminology, and social harm. Allison is actively researching: Food as both environmental harm and as solutions to environmental harm; the intersection of violence against humans and animals; consumer-based (food) activism; the socio-ecological role of plant-meat; and the governance of food choice. Allison's dissertation explores perceptions of the role of plant-meat in contributing to environmental harm, and her recent edited book *A Handbook of Food Crime* brings a criminal gaze to the world of food production and consumption.

Alaina Interisano is a doctorate student at York University in the Faculty of Environmental Studies. She obtained her BA and MA in sociology at Brock University, concentrating in critical animal studies. Her current research interests center around the convergence of environmental education and critical animal pedagogy, and human-animal relations in science education and research. For her dissertation research, she will explore the implementation of humane education principles and non-animal alternative methods and technologies in post-secondary science education.

Kenzo Jacquemin studies anthropology at Université de Liège in Belgium. He is working on the links between anarchism and antispeciesism, on the 269 Libération Animale's sanctuary, on the rats in town and on Islamic thoughts about animals.

Maryline El Khoury studies political sociology at Université Paris 1 Panthéon-Sorbonne in Paris. She is working on the emergence of slaughterhouses in Paris in the XIXth century with a perspective from below, from the oppressed.

Kati Lewis is an Associate Professor of English at Salt Lake Community College. There is no hierarchy to the following ways of being that Lewis inhabits her body and mind. She's a teacher, lover, activist, mother, hiker, sometimes marathoner, and need-to-find-more-time-for-writing writer. As a sexual violence survivor and bisexual womxn raised in a very patriarchal religion, her teaching and writing investigate the myriad sociopolitical and environmental experiences of intersectional identities, stories, and histories. Three of the major frameworks for her research, teaching, and writing are exploring themes of silence and voice in the United States, the power and importance of real representation, and the necessity of unerasing intersectional LGBTQ+ histories.

Anthony J. Nocella II, Ph.D., scholar-activist and co-founder of critical animal studies, radical animal studies, terrorization, disability pedagogy, lowrider studies, and Hip Hop criminology, is an Assistant Professor in the Department of Criminal Justice and Criminology in the Institute of Public Safety at Salt Lake Community College. He is the editor of the Peace Studies Journal, Transformative Justice Journal, and co-editor of five book series including Critical Animal Studies and Theory with Lexington Books and Hip Hop Studies and Activism with Peter Lang Publishing. He is the National Director of Save the Kids and Executive Director of the Institute for Critical Animal Studies. He has published over fifty book chapters or articles and forty books. He has been interviewed by New York Times, Washington Post, Houston Chronicles, Fresno Bee, Fox, CBS, CNN, C-SPAN, and Los Angeles Times.

Sean Parson, Ph.D., is an Assistant Professor in the departments of Politics and International Affairs and Sustainable Communities at Northern Arizona University. They are the author of the book *Cooking Up a Revolution: Food Not Bombs, Homes Not Jails, and Resistance to Gentrification* (Manchester University Press, 2018) and the co-editor of *Superheroes and Critical Animal Studies: The Heroic Beasts of Total Liberation* (Lexington Academic Press, 2017), *A historical Scholarly Collection of the Writings on the Earth Liberation Front* (Peter Lang, 2019), *Representations of Political Resistance and Emancipation of Science Fiction* (Lexington Press, 2020). They have published in *Theory and Event, New Political Science, Capitalism Socialism and Nature* and other academic journals.

Nathan Poirier is a doctorate student in Sociology with specializations in critical animal studies and women's and *gender* studies. He is co-director of students for critical animal studies. Nathan has a wide array of academic interests, but his main interests include intersectionality, anarchism, animals, veganism, human overpopulation, resource consumption, radical social movements, and critical pedagogy. Nathan has been teaching math at the college level since 2012 and enjoys integrating social responsibility and justice into his classrooms. In 2015 he organized a community-focused rewilding event in Grand Rapids, MI.

Sarah Tomasello received her B.A. in Anthropology and Religious Studies and has a master's degree in Anthrozoology from Canisius College. She is especially interested in the intersections between decolonization, animal rights, feminism and wildlife conservation. More specifically, she hopes to learn about the importance of Traditional Ecological Knowledge to conservation initiatives, and how methodologies can be improved so that conservationists can work more respectfully with Indigenous communities. She is also intrigued by more-than-human ethnography, and research which aims to understand the realities of the nonhuman species most marginalized by human society, such as those labeled as "pests."

Index

RADICAL ANIMAL STUDIES AND TOTAL LIBERATION

Anthony J. Nocella II, SERIES EDITOR

The **Radical Animal Studies and Total Liberation** book series branches out of Critical Animal Studies (a field co-founded by Anthony J. Nocella II) with the argument that criticism is not enough. Action must follow theory. This series demands that scholars are engaged with their subjects both theoretically and actively via radical, revolutionary, intersectional action for total liberation. Founded in anarchism, the series provides space for scholar-activists who challenge authoritarianism and oppression in their many daily forms. **Radical Animal Studies and Total Liberation** promotes accessible and inclusive scholarship that is based on personal narrative as well as traditional research, and is especially interested in the advancement of interwoven voices and perspectives from multiple radical, revolutionary social justice groups and movements such as Black Lives Matter, Idle No More, Earth First!, the Zapatistas, ADAPT, prison abolition, LGBTTQQIA rights, disability liberation, Earth Liberation Front, Animal Liberation Front, political prisoners, radical transnational feminism, environmental justice, food justice, youth justice, and Hip Hop activism.

To order other books in this series please contact our Customer Service Department:

PETERLANG@PRESSWAREHOUSE.COM (WITHIN THE U.S.)

ORDERS@PETERLANG.COM (OUTSIDE THE U.S.)

To find out more about the series or browse a full list of titles, please visit our website:

WWW.PETERLANG.COM

www.ingramcontent.com/pod-product-compliance
Lightning Source LLC
Chambersburg PA
CBHW050522280326
41932CB00014B/2423